5000 FRENCH WORDS

**Essential Vocabulary
for Examinations**

COLLINS
GEM

5000 FRENCH WORDS

Barbara I. Christie

HarperCollinsPublishers

first published in this edition 1991

© William Collins Sons & Co. Ltd. 1979
© HarperCollins Publishers 1991

latest reprint 1997

ISBN 0 00 471002-9 Paperback

Based on 5000 French Words © 1979,
compiled by Barbara I. Christie MA (Hons)
and Màiri MacGinn MA (Hons)

Printed and bound in Great Britain by
Caledonian International Book Manufacturing Ltd,
Glasgow, G64

Whether you are revising for school exams or whether, as an adult user, you want to brush up your French vocabulary, this book offers you the information you require in a helpful and accessible format.

The main part of the book comprises 50 topics, covering such common vocabulary areas as ANIMALS, GREETINGS, HEALTH, SHOPPING and the WEATHER. These are given in alphabetical order, in double-page spreads.

Vocabulary within each topic is divided into the relevant nouns for that topic, in alphabetical order, followed by appropriate adjectives, verbs, example phrases and constructions. These will help you to produce the kind of sentences you need in everyday communication.

All masculine nouns are given on left-hand pages, and all feminine nouns on right-hand pages, to make it easier to associate nouns with their gender. In addition, vocabulary within each topic is graded, so that you can choose what to cover according to your particular requirements. ESSENTIAL vocabulary includes the basics for communication on a given topic, IMPORTANT items expand on this, and USEFUL material increases the depth with which you will be able to express yourself.

This arrangement is particularly helpful for GCSE revision, since ESSENTIAL vocabulary covers the minimum requirements for GCSE at Basic level. If in addition you learn the IMPORTANT vocabulary, you will have covered everything you need for GCSE at Higher level.

Two symbols are used in the topics sections. The book symbol ⌑ indicates words which you must be able to recognize without necessarily being able to use yourself. This symbol is used to mark vocabulary in both the ESSENTIAL and IMPORTANT categories but all GCSE students at Higher level must treat items of ESSENTIAL vocabulary so marked as if they had no symbol: you must know them actively, not just for comprehension.

The arrow symbol ⇔ shows that the word so marked can have another meaning, either in the same topic or in a completely different one. There is a list of these words at the end of the book, entitled HOMONYMS.

Of course a knowledge of French doesn't begin and end with memorizing individual words, and this is where the phrases and idioms come into their own. These are just the sorts of expressions you will be likely to hear and will want to produce for yourself.

The second section of the book groups words according to part of speech — adjective, conjunction, noun etc — to provide you with a useful checklist. This includes words which can be used with most or even all the topics — the type of vocabulary which you will come across in everyday situations and which is not confined to one particular topic.

All feminine forms of adjectives are shown, as are irregular plurals and plurals of compound nouns. The swung dash ~ is used to indicate the basic elements of the compound and appropriate endings are then added, e.g. at FARM there is **la moissonneuse-batteuse** (pl ~s~s) and at FREE TIME there is **le week-end** (pl ~s).

French has a certain number of nouns which have one form regardless of whether they are referring to a male or a female. This book shows these with (m+f), e.g. **le professeur** (m+f) and **la vedette** (m+f).

Finally, there is an English index which covers all the ESSENTIAL and IMPORTANT nouns given under the topic headings.

ABBREVIATIONS

adj	adjective	*n*	noun
adv	adverb	*pl*	plural
conj	conjunction	*prep*	preposition
f	feminine	*qch*	quelque chose
inv	invariable	*qn*	quelqu'un
m	masculine	*sb*	somebody
m+f	masculine and	*sth*	something
	feminine form	*subj*	subjunctive

PHONETICS

i	as in **vie**, **lit**	ɛ̃	as in m**atin**, pl**ein**
e	as in bl**é**, jou**er**	ɑ̃	as in s**ans**, v**ent**
ɛ	as in m**erci**, tr**ès**	ɔ̃	as in b**on**, **ombre**
a	as in p**atte**, pl**at**	œ̃	as in br**un**, l**undi**
ɑ	as in b**as**, gr**as**	j	as in **yeux**, p**ied**
ɔ	as in m**ort**, d**onner**	ɥ	as in l**ui**, h**uile**
o	as in m**ot**, g**auche**	ɲ	as in **agneau**, v**igne**
u	as in gen**ou**, r**oue**	ŋ	as in English -**ing**
y	as in r**ue**, t**u**	ʃ	as in **chat**, ta**che**
ø	as in p**eu**, d**eux**	ʒ	as in **je**, g**ens**
œ	as in p**eur**, m**euble**	ʀ	as in **rue**, veni**r**
ə	as in l**e**, pr**emier**		

A colon : precedes words beginning with an aspirate
h (**le :hibou** as opposed to **l'hippopotame**).

CONTENTS 8

ESSENTIAL WORDS (m)	
l'air ✧	air
un aller-retour	return ticket
un aller (simple)	single ticket
un avion	plane, aeroplane
les bagages	luggage
le billet ✧ (d'avion)	(plane) ticket
le bureau de renseignements	information desk
le départ ▭	departure
le douanier ▭	customs officer
l'horaire ▭	timetable
le numéro	number
les objets trouvés	lost and found
le passager	passenger
le passeport	passport
le plan ✧	plan, map
le porteur ▭	porter
le prix du billet	fare
les renseignements ✧	information
le retard	delay
le sac	bag
le tarif ✧	rate, fare
le taxi	taxi
le touriste	tourist
le voyageur ▭	traveller, passenger

voyager par avion to travel by plane, to fly
retenir une place d'avion to book a plane ticket
(envoyer une lettre) par avion (to send a letter) by airmail
enregistrer ses bagages to check in one's luggage
j'ai manqué l'avion/la correspondance I missed my plane/my connection
l'avion a décollé/a atterri the plane has taken off/ has landed

---

ESSENTIAL WORDS (f)

une agence de voyages	travel agent's
une arrivée 🗀	arrival
la consigne	left luggage office
la consigne automatique 🗀	left luggage locker
la correspondance 🗀	connection
la descente	descent
la douane 🗀	customs
une entrée ◇	entrance
l'hôtesse de l'air	air hostess
la passagère	passenger
la réduction	reduction
la réservation 🗀	reservation
la sortie	exit
la sortie de secours ◇ 🗀	emergency exit
les toilettes	toilet(s)
la touriste	tourist
la valise	case, suitcase

le tableau des arrivées/des départs the arrivals/ departures board

le vol numéro 776 en provenance de Nice/à destination de Nice flight number 776 from Nice/ to Nice

récupérer ses bagages to get one's luggage back

quand je passe à la douane when I go through Customs

j'ai quelque chose à déclarer I have something to declare

je n'ai rien à déclarer I have nothing to declare

fouiller les bagages to search the luggage

les bagages à main hand luggage

IMPORTANT WORDS (m)

un accident d'avion	air *or* plane crash
un aéroport	airport
le chariot	(luggage) trolley
un escalier roulant ▭	escalator
l'hélicoptère	helicopter
l'homme d'affaires	businessman
le mal de l'air	airsickness
le pilote ⇨	pilot
le vol ⇨	flying; flight

USEFUL WORDS (m)

un aiguilleur du ciel	air traffic controller
un atterrissage	landing
un avion à réaction	jet plane
un avion gros porteur	jumbo jet
le décollage	take-off
l'embarquement	boarding
un équipage	crew
un indicateur	timetable
le mur du son	sound barrier
le parachute	parachute
le radar	radar
le satellite	satellite terminal
le steward	steward
le tapis roulant	moving walkway
le trou d'air	air pocket
le vacancier	holiday-maker

à bord de l'avion on board the plane
"éteignez vos cigarettes" "extinguish your
cigarettes"
"attachez vos ceintures" "fasten your seat belts"
nous survolons Londres we are flying over London
mon ami a le mal de l'air my friend is feeling
airsick
détourner un avion to hijack a plane

IMPORTANT WORDS (f)

la ceinture de sécurité
        seat belt
la destination   destination
la durée   length, duration
l'horloge   (large) clock
la salle de départ   departure lounge
la vitesse ♢   speed

USEFUL WORDS (f)

une aérogare   air terminal; airport
           building
une aile   wing
une altitude   altitude
une ascension   climb
les balises de nuit   runway lights
la boîte noire   black box
les commandes   controls
une escale   stop-over
une étiquette   label
la :hauteur   height
l'hélice   propeller
la ligne aérienne   airline
la piste ♢ **(d'envol)** runway
la tour de contrôle control tower
la turbulence   turbulence

nous allons faire escale à New York we shall stop
  over in New York
un atterrissage forcé a forced landing, an
  emergency landing
un atterrissage en catastrophe a crash landing
les droits (*mpl*) **de douane** customs duty
exempté(e) de douane duty-free
le magasin hors-taxe the duty-free shop
des cigarettes hors-taxe duty-free cigarettes

ESSENTIAL WORDS (m)

un animal (pl animaux)	animal
le bœuf ◇ [bœf]	
(pl ~s [bø])	ox
le chat	cat
le cheval (pl chevaux)	horse
le chien	dog
le cochon	pig
un éléphant	elephant
le :hamster	hamster
le lapin ▭	rabbit
le lion	lion
le mouton ◇	sheep
un oiseau (pl -x)	bird
le poisson	fish
le tigre	tiger
le zoo [zoo]	zoo

IMPORTANT WORDS (m)

le cou	neck
le jardin zoologique	zoo

aimer to like; **détester** to hate; **préférer** to prefer

j'aime les chats, je déteste les serpents, je préfère les souris I like cats, I hate snakes, I prefer mice

nous avons 12 animaux chez nous we have 12 pets in our house

nous n'avons pas d'animaux chez nous we have no pets (in our house)

les animaux sauvages wild animals

les animaux domestiques pets, household animals

j'aime faire du cheval or **monter à cheval** I like horse-riding

à cheval on horseback

"attention chien méchant" "beware of the dog"

"chiens interdits" "no dogs allowed"

"bas les pattes!" (to dog) "down!"

ESSENTIAL WORDS (f)

la bouche	mouth (*of horse, sheep, cow*)
la chatte	(she-)cat
la chienne	(she-)dog, bitch
la fourrure	fur
une oreille	ear
la souris	mouse
la tortue	tortoise
la vache	cow

IMPORTANT WORDS (f)

la cage	cage
la queue ▷ [kø]	tail

grand(e) big; **petit(e)** little
gros(se) fat; **mince** thin
beau (*and* **bel** *before a vowel or aspirate h*)
  (belle) beautiful, handsome
laid(e) ugly
joli(e) nice
intelligent(e) intelligent
nerveux(euse) nervous
timide timid

le chien aboie the dog barks; **il grogne** it growls
le chat miaule the cat miaows; **il ronronne** it purrs

USEFUL WORDS (m)

un **âne**	donkey
les **bois**	antlers
le **bouc**	(billy) goat
le **cerf** [sɛʀ]	deer, stag
le **chameau** (pl -x)	camel
le **cobaye**	guinea-pig
le **crapaud**	toad
le **crocodile**	crocodile
un **écureuil**	squirrel
le **:hérisson**	hedgehog
l'**hippopotame**	hippopotamus
le **kangourou**	kangaroo
le **lièvre**	hare
le **loup**	wolf
le **mulet**	mule
le **museau** (pl -x)	snout (of pig)
un **ours** [uʀs]	bear
un **ours blanc**	polar bear
le **phasme**	stick insect
le **phoque**	seal
le **piège**	trap
les **piquants**	spines (of hedgehog)
le **poil**	coat, hair
le **poney**	pony
le **porc** ⇨ [pɔʀ]	pig
le **protestataire**	protester
le **renard**	fox
le **rhinocéros**	rhinoceros
le **sabot**	hoof
le **serpent**	snake
le **singe**	monkey
le **taureau** (pl -x)	bull
le **zèbre**	zebra

mettre un animal en cage to put an animal in a cage
libérer un animal to set an animal free

USEFUL WORDS (f)

la baleine	whale
la bosse	hump (*of camel*)
la boutique d'animaux	pet shop
la caractéristique	characteristic
la carapace	shell (*of tortoise*)
la chauve-souris (*pl ~s~*)	bat
la chèvre	(nanny-)goat
la corne	horn
la couleuvre	grass snake
la crinière	mane (*of lion, horse*)
la défense ⟡	tusk
une expérience ⟡	experiment
la fourrure	fur
la girafe	giraffe
la grenouille	frog
la griffe	claw
la gueule	mouth (*of dog, cat, lion etc*)
la jument	mare
la lionne	lioness
la mule	mule
la patte	paw
la poche ⟡	pouch (*of kangaroo*)
la ramure	antlers
les rayures	stripes (*of zebra*)
la taupe	mole
la tigresse	tigress
la trompe	trunk (*of elephant*)

faire des expériences sur des animaux to do experiments on animals
les droits des animaux animal rights

ESSENTIAL WORDS (m)

le casque ⌑	helmet
le cyclisme ⌑	cycling
le cycliste ⌑	cyclist
le frein ⌑	brake
le pneu	tyre
le Tour de France	Tour de France cycle race
le vélo ⬦	bike; cycling

IMPORTANT WORDS (m)

le sommet	top (*of hill*)

USEFUL WORDS (m)

le catadioptre	reflector
le cataphote	reflector
le cuissard	cycle pants *or* shorts
le garde-boue (*pl inv*)	mudguard
le guidon	handlebars
le moyeu (*pl* -x)	hub
le pare-boue (*pl inv*)	mud flap
le porte-bagages (*pl inv*)	luggage rack
le rayon ⬦	spoke
le réflecteur	reflector
le timbre ⬦	bell
le vélo tout terrain	mountain bike

marcher to walk; **aller à pied** to go on foot
aller à bicyclette, aller à *or* **en vélo** to go by bike
je suis venu(e) en vélo I came by bike, I came on my bike
vous pouvez y aller à vélo you can go there on your bike, you can cycle there
faire du cyclisme, faire du vélo to go in for cycling
rouler to travel; **à toute vitesse** at full speed
s'arrêter to stop
freiner brusquement to brake sharply

ESSENTIAL WORDS (f)	
la bicyclette 🕮	bicycle
la lampe	lamp

IMPORTANT WORDS (f)	
la crevaison	puncture
la roue	wheel
la vitesse ⇨	speed; gear

USEFUL WORDS (f)	
la barre	crossbar
la chaîne	chain
la côte ⇨	slope, hill (on road)
la dynamo	dynamo
la pédale	pedal
la pente	slope
la piste cyclable	cycle path
la pompe	pump
la sacoche ⇨ (de bicyclette)**	saddlebag, pannier
la selle	saddle
la sonnette	bell
la trousse de secours pour crevaisons	puncture repair kit
la valve	valve

monter à bicyclette to get on one's bike
faire une promenade à *or* **en bicyclette** to go for a bike ride
être à plat to have a flat tyre
réparer un pneu crevé to mend a puncture
la roue avant/arrière the front/back wheel
gonfler les pneus to blow up the tyres
brillant(e), reluisant(e) shiny; **rouillé(e)** rusty
fluorescent(e) fluorescent

ESSENTIAL WORDS (m)	
le canard	duck
le ciel 🕮	sky
le coq	cock
le dindon	turkey
un oiseau (pl -x)	bird
le perroquet	parrot
le poulet	chicken

USEFUL WORDS (m)	
un aigle	eagle
le bec	beak
le choucas	jackdaw
le coq de bruyère	grouse
le corbeau (pl -x)	raven
le coucou	cuckoo
le cygne [sin]	swan
un étourneau (pl -x)	starling
le faisan	pheasant
le faucon	falcon, hawk
le flamant (rose)	(pink) flamingo
le :hibou (pl -x)	owl
le mainate	mynah bird
le martin-pêcheur (pl ~s~s)	kingfisher
le merle	blackbird
le moineau (pl -x)	sparrow
le nid	nest
le paon [pã]	peacock
le pic ⬦	woodpecker
le pigeon	pigeon
le pingouin	penguin
le roitelet	wren
le rossignol	nightingale
le rouge-gorge (pl ~s~s)	robin (redbreast)
le serin	canary
le vautour	vulture

ESSENTIAL WORDS (f)

une oie 🕮	goose
la perruche	budgie, budgerigar
la poule 🕮	hen

USEFUL WORDS (f)

une aile	wing
une alouette	lark
une autruche	ostrich
la cage	cage
la caille	quail
la cigogne	stork
la colombe	dove
la corneille	crow, raven
la grive	thrush
la grouse	grouse
l'hirondelle	swallow
la mésange bleue	bluetit
la mouette	seagull
la perdrix [pɛʀdʀi]	partridge
la pie	magpie
la plume	feather

voler to fly; **s'envoler** to fly away
les oiseaux volent dans l'air birds fly in the air
ils font des nids they build nests
ils sifflent they whistle; **ils chantent** they sing
on les met en cage people put them in cages

ESSENTIAL WORDS (m)

le bras	arm
les cheveux	hair
le cœur 📖	heart
le corps [kɔr] 📖	body
le côté	side
le doigt	finger
le dos	back
l'estomac [ɛstɔma] 📖	stomach
le genou (*pl* **-x**)	knee
le nez	nose
un œil (*pl* **yeux**)	eye
le pied	foot
le ventre	stomach
le visage 📖	face
les yeux	eyes

IMPORTANT WORDS (m)

le cou	neck
le front	forehead
le menton	chin
le pouce	thumb
le sang 📖	blood
le sourcil [sursi]	eyebrow

debout standing; **assis(e)** sitting; **couché(e)** lying
je me suis cassé le bras/la jambe I have broken
  my arm/my leg
je me suis coupé le doigt I have cut my finger
je vais me faire couper les cheveux I am going to
  have my hair cut
son cœur battait his *or* her heart was beating
jeter un coup d'œil à qn to glance at sb
en un clin d'œil in the twinkling of an eye
(j'y vais) à pied (I'm going) on foot
un coup de pied a kick
il m'a donné un coup de pied he kicked me

ESSENTIAL WORDS (f)	
la bouche	mouth
la dent	tooth
la gorge	throat
la jambe	leg
la main	hand
une oreille	ear
la tête	head

IMPORTANT WORDS (f)	
la cheville 📖	ankle
une épaule	shoulder
la figure	face
la joue	cheek
la langue ▷	tongue
la peau 📖	skin
la poitrine 📖	chest, bust
la voix	voice

ouvrir/fermer la bouche to open/close one's mouth
se taire to keep quiet; **taisez-vous!, tais-toi!** be quiet!
j'ai mal à la gorge I have a sore throat
j'ai mal au ventre I have a sore stomach, I've got stomach ache
ils se sont serré la main they shook hands
de la tête aux pieds from head to foot
lever la tête or **les yeux** to look up
je me suis foulé la cheville I have sprained my ankle
"tour de poitrine" "chest or bust measurement"
parlez plus fort! speak louder!

USEFUL WORDS (m)

le cerveau	brain
le cil [sil]	eyelash
le coude	elbow
le derrière	bottom
les doigts de pied	toes
le foie	liver
le geste	gesture, movement
le gros orteil	the big toe
un index	forefinger
le mollet	calf (of leg)
le muscle	muscle
un ongle	nail
un orteil	toe
un os [ɔs] (pl [o])	bone
le poignet	wrist
le poing	fist
le poumon	lung
le rein	kidney
le sein	breast
le squelette	skeleton
le talon	heel
le teint	complexion
le trait	feature

sourd(e) deaf; **aveugle** blind; **muet(te)** dumb
handicapé(e) handicapped; **handicapé(e)**
  mental(e) mentally handicapped
un coup de poing a punch
il m'a donné un coup de poing he punched me
à pleins poumons at the top of one's voice

USEFUL WORDS (f)

une **artère**	artery
la **chair**	flesh
la **colonne vertébrale**	spine
la **côte** ▷	rib
la **cuisse**	thigh
la **:hanche**	hip
la **lèvre**	lip
la **mâchoire**	jaw
la **nuque**	nape of the neck
la **paupière**	eyelid
la **plante du pied**	sole of the foot
la **prunelle**	pupil (of the eye)
la **taille** ▷	figure; waist
la **tempe**	temple
la **veine** ▷	vein

"tour de hanches" "hip measurement"
"tour de taille" "waist measurement"

THE SEASONS

le printemps	spring
l'été (*m*)	summer
l'automne (*m*)	autumn
l'hiver (*m*)	winter

au printemps in spring
en été/automne/hiver in summer/autumn/winter

THE MONTHS

janvier	January	**juillet**	July
février	February	**août**	August
mars	March	**septembre**	September
avril	April	**octobre**	October
mai	May	**novembre**	November
juin	June	**décembre**	December

en mai *etc,* **au mois de mai** *etc* in May *etc*
le premier avril April Fools' Day
le premier mai May Day
le quatorze juillet Bastille Day (*French national holiday*)
le quinze août Assumption (*French national holiday*)

THE DAYS OF THE WEEK

lundi	Monday
mardi	Tuesday
mercredi	Wednesday
jeudi	Thursday
vendredi	Friday
samedi	Saturday
dimanche	Sunday

le samedi *etc* on Saturdays *etc*
samedi *etc* on Saturday *etc*
samedi *etc* **prochain/dernier** next/last Saturday *etc*
le samedi *etc* **précédent/suivant** the previous/following Saturday *etc*

le calendrier	the calendar
la saison	the season
le mois	the month
les jours de la semaine	the days of the week
le jour férié	public holiday

le dimanche des Rameaux/de Pâques Palm/ Easter Sunday
le lundi de Pâques/de Pentecôte Easter/Whit Monday
Mardi gras Shrove *or* Pancake Tuesday
mercredi des Cendres Ash Wednesday
le jeudi de l'Ascension Ascension Day
le vendredi saint Good Friday
le jour de l'An New Year's Day
le réveillon du jour de l'an New Year's Eve dinner *or* party
le jour J D-Day
le jour des Morts All Souls' Day
le jour des Rois Epiphany, Twelfth Night
l'Avent (*m*) Advent
le Carême Lent
la Marseillaise the Marseillaise (*French national anthem*)
Noël (*m*) Christmas
à (la) Noël at Christmas
le jour de Noël Christmas Day
la veille de Noël, la nuit de Noël Christmas Eve
le lendemain de Noël Boxing Day
Pâques (*fpl*) Easter
le jour de Pâques Easter Day
Pâque (*f*) **juive** Passover
le poisson d'avril April fool; April fool's trick
la Saint-Sylvestre New Year's Eve, Hogmanay
la Saint-Valentin St. Valentine's Day
la Toussaint All Saints' Day
la veille de la Toussaint Hallowe'en
le drapeau tricolore the (French) tricolour

ESSENTIAL WORDS (m)

un anniversaire	birthday
un anniversaire de mariage	wedding anniversary
le bal	dance
le cadeau (*pl* -x)	present
le divorce	divorce
le mariage	marriage, wedding
le rendez-vous (*pl inv*)	appointment, date

IMPORTANT WORDS (m)

le cirque ⮧	circus
le drapeau (*pl* -x)	flag
le festival	festival
le feu d'artifice	firework; firework display
le feu de joie	bonfire

USEFUL WORDS (m)

le baptême	christening, baptism
le char fleuri	decorated float
le cimetière	cemetery, churchyard
les confettis	confetti
le décès	death
le défilé	procession; march
un enterrement	funeral, burial
le faire-part (de mariage) (*pl inv*)	wedding announcement/ invitation
le témoin du marié	best man

---

célébrer *or* **fêter son anniversaire** to celebrate one's birthday
elle vient d'avoir ses 17 ans she's just (turned) 17
le bal du Nouvel An the New Year's Eve dance
il m'a offert ce cadeau he gave me this present
je te l'offre! I'm giving it to you!
je vous remercie thank you (very much)
divorcer to get divorced; **se marier** to get married

ESSENTIAL WORDS (f)

la date	date
la fête	saint's day; fête, fair

IMPORTANT WORDS (f)

les festivités	festivities
la fête foraine	(fun) fair
les fiançailles 🔲	engagement
la foire	(fun) fair
la mort ♢	death
la naissance	birth

USEFUL WORDS (f)

la cérémonie	ceremony
la demoiselle d'honneur	bridesmaid
les étrennes	New Year's gift; Christmas box
la fanfare ♢	brass band; fanfare
la fête folklorique	festival of folk music
la lune de miel	honeymoon
les noces	wedding
la retraite	retirement

se fiancer (avec qn) to get engaged (to sb)
mon père est mort il y a deux ans my father died two years ago
enterrer, ensevelir to bury
ma sœur est née en 1985 my sister was born in 1985
aller à la noce de qn to go to sb's wedding
les noces d'argent/d'or/de diamant silver/golden/diamond wedding
soyez le *or* **la bienvenu(e)** *(pl* **les bienvenu(e)s)** you are very welcome
souhaiter la bonne année à qn to wish sb a happy New Year

ESSENTIAL WORDS (m)

un **arbre**	tree
le **bac à vaisselle** ⮐	washing-up bowl
le **bloc sanitaire** ⮐	washrooms
le **bol**	bowl
le **campeur**	camper
le **camping**	camping; camp-site
le **couteau** (*pl* **-x**)	knife
le **dépôt de butane** ⮐	butane store
un **emplacement** ⮐	pitch, site
le **feu de camp**	camp-fire
le **gardien** ⇨ ⮐	warden, attendant
le **gaz**	gas
le **lavabo**	washbasin
le **lit de camp**	camp bed
les **plats cuisinés** ⮐	cooked meals
le **rasoir** ⮐	razor
le **supplément** ⮐	extra charge
le **terrain (de camping)** ⮐	camp-site
le **véhicule** ⮐	vehicle
le **verre**	glass
les **W.-C.** ⮐	toilet(s)

IMPORTANT WORDS (m)

le **matelas pneumatique**	airbed, lilo
un **ouvre-boîte(s)**	tin-opener
le **réchaud**	stove
le **règlement**	rule
le **sac à dos**	backpack, rucksack
le **sac de couchage**	sleeping bag
le **tire-bouchon** (*pl* ~**s**)	corkscrew

---

faire du camping to go camping; **camper** to camp
bien aménagé(e) well equipped
monter to set up; **mettre** to put; **débarrasser** to
 clear up

ESSENTIAL WORDS (f)

une allumette	match
une assiette	plate
la boîte	tin, can; box
les boîtes de conserve	tinned food
la campeuse	camper
la caravane	caravan
la carte ◇	map; card
la chaise (longue)	(deck) chair
la cuiller, cuillère	spoon
la cuisinière ◇ **(à gaz)**	
🕮	(gas) cooker or stove
la douche	shower
l'eau (potable)	(drinking) water
la fourchette	fork
la glace ◇	mirror
la lampe électrique	torch
la machine à laver 🕮	washing machine
la nuit	night
la piscine	swimming pool
la poubelle	dustbin
la salle ◇ 🕮	room; hall
la table	table
la tasse	cup
la tente	tent
les toilettes	toilet(s)

IMPORTANT WORDS (f)

les installations sanitaires 🕮	washing facilities
la laverie	launderette, laundry
la lessive	washing powder; washing
l'ombre	shade; shadow
la prise de courant 🕮	socket, power point
la salle de jeux 🕮	games room

dresser une tente to pitch a tent
dormir to sleep; **se réveiller** to wake up

ESSENTIAL WORDS (m)

un **agent (de police)**	policeman
le **bureau** ◊ (pl -x)	office
le **chauffeur de taxi** 🕮	taxi driver
un **électricien** 🕮	electrician
un **employé** ◊ 🕮	employee; clerk
un **employeur** 🕮	employer
le **facteur** 🕮	postman
le **garagiste** 🕮	mechanic; garage owner
un **infirmier** 🕮	(male) nurse
le **laitier**	milkman
le **mécanicien** ◊ 🕮	mechanic; engineer; train-driver
le **médecin** (m+f)	doctor
le **métier** 🕮	trade
le **mineur**	miner
le **patron** ◊	boss
le **pharmacien**	chemist
le **pompier** 🕮	fireman
le **professeur** (m+f)	teacher
le **roi**	king
le **salaire** 🕮	salary, pay, wages
le **secrétaire** ◊ 🕮	secretary
le **soldat**	soldier
le **travail**	work
le **vendeur** 🕮	salesman, shop assistant

intéressant(e)/peu intéressant(e) interesting/not very interesting

se mettre au travail to start work, get down to work

il est facteur, c'est un facteur he is a postman

il/elle est médecin, c'est un médecin he/she is a doctor

il est facteur de son métier he is a postman by trade *or* to trade

---

ESSENTIAL WORDS (f)

une ambition	ambition
la banque	bank
la dactylo(graphe)	typist
une employée ⟡ ▭	employee
la factrice ▭	postwoman
l'hôtesse de l'air	air hostess
une industrie ▭	industry
une infirmière ▭	nurse
la patronne ⟡	boss
la profession ▭	profession
la réceptionniste ▭	receptionist
la reine	queen
la secrétaire ⟡ ▭	secretary
une usine	factory
la vedette ⟡ (*m+f*)	star
la vendeuse ▭	salesgirl, shop assistant
la vie	life

travailler to work; **devenir** to become

travailler pour gagner sa vie to work to earn one's living

mon ambition est d'être secrétaire, j'ai l'ambition d'être secrétaire it is my ambition to be a secretary

que faites-vous dans la vie? what work do you do?, what is your job?

IMPORTANT WORDS (m)

un auteur	author
l'avenir	future
le chef ⟡ (m+f)	boss
le chômage	unemployment
le chômeur	unemployed person
le coiffeur	hairdresser; barber
le collègue	colleague
le commerçant ⌑	tradesman
le commerce	commerce, business
le concierge	caretaker; janitor
le décorateur	decorator
un emploi	job
le gérant	manager
l'homme d'affaires	businessman
un opticien	optician
un ouvrier	worker
le pilote ⟡	pilot; racing driver
le plombier	plumber
le premier ministre (m+f)	prime minister
le président	president; chairman
le salarié	wage-earner
le sapeur-pompier (pl ~s~s)	fireman
le syndicat ⌑	trade union
les syndiqués	union members

être au chômage to be out of work, be unemployed
mettre qn en or **au chômage** to make sb redundant
"demandes d'emplois" "situations wanted"
"offres d'emplois" "situations vacant"
je vais faire une demande d'emploi I am going to apply for a job

IMPORTANT WORDS (f)

les affaires ◇	business
une augmentation ▢	rise
la bibliothèque ◇	library
la carrière ◇ ▢	career
la coiffeuse ◇	hairdresser
la collègue	colleague
la concierge	caretaker
la cuisinière ◇	cook
une entrevue	interview
la femme d'affaires	businesswoman
la femme de ménage	cleaning woman
la gérante ▢	manageress
la grève	strike
l'intention	intention, aim
une ouvreuse	usherette
une ouvrière	worker
la politique	politics
la présidente	president; chairwoman
la salariée	wage-earner
la situation ▢	job, situation

gagner/toucher £150 par semaine to earn/get £150 a week

une augmentation de salaire a wage or pay rise

se mettre en grève to go on strike

faire la grève to be on strike

travailler à plein temps/à mi-temps to work full-time/part-time

faire des heures supplémentaires to work overtime

USEFUL WORDS (m)

un architecte [aʀʃitɛkt(ə)]	architect
un artiste	artist
un avocat ◇	barrister
un avoué	solicitor
le cadre ◇	executive
le chercheur	researcher
le chirurgien	surgeon
le comptable	accountant
le constructeur	builder
le cosmonaute	cosmonaut, astronaut
le couturier	fashion designer
le député	M.P., member of parliament
un écrivain	writer
le fonctionnaire	civil servant
l'homme politique	politician
un ingénieur	engineer
un interprète	interpreter
le journaliste	journalist
le juge	judge
le maçon	mason
le mannequin ◇ (m+f)	model (person)
le marin	sailor; seaman
le menuisier	joiner
le notaire	lawyer, solicitor
le personnel	staff
le photographe	photographer
le président-directeur général, PDG	chairman and managing director
le prêtre	priest
le représentant	representative
le speaker [spikœr]	announcer
le stage	(training) course
le traitement	salary
le vétérinaire (m+f)	vet(erinary surgeon)
le vigneron	wine grower

USEFUL WORDS (f)	
l'administration	administration
une artiste	artist
une avocate	lawyer
la compagnie	company
la comptable	accountant
la couturière	dressmaker
la dispute	argument, dispute
une entreprise	business
la femme-agent	policewoman
la femme au foyer	housewife
la firme	firm
la formation	training
la grève du zèle	work-to-rule
la grève perlée	go-slow
une interprète	interpreter
la journaliste	journalist
la maison de	
commerce	firm
l'orientation	
professionnelle	careers guidance
la religieuse	nun
la speakerine [spikʀin]	announcer
la sténo-	
dactylo(graphe)	shorthand typist

un emploi temporaire/permanent a temporary/
  permanent job
être engagé(e) to be taken on
être renvoyé(e) to be dismissed
mettre qn à la porte to give sb the sack

ESSENTIAL WORDS *(m)*

un agent (de police)	policeman
l'auto-stop	hitch-hiking
un auto-stoppeur	
(pl ~s)	hitch-hiker
le camion	lorry, truck
le carrefour	crossroads
le chauffeur ⟫ *(m+f)*	driver; chauffeur
le conducteur ⌑	driver
le cycliste ⌑	cyclist
le feu rouge ⌑	traffic lights, red light
les feux (de circulation)	traffic lights
le frein ⌑	brake
le garage	garage
le garagiste ⌑	mechanic; garage owner
le gas-oil ⌑	diesel (oil)
le kilomètre	kilometre
le litre	litre
le mécanicien ⟫ ⌑	mechanic
le numéro	number
le parking ⟫	car park
le péage ⌑	toll
le permis de conduire ⌑	driving licence
le piéton	pedestrian
le plan ⟫ **(de la ville)**	street map
le pneu	tyre
le super	4-star petrol
le voyage	journey

faire de l'auto-stop to go hitch-hiking
déposer un auto-stoppeur to drop off a hitch-hiker
s'arrêter au feu rouge to stop at the red light
freiner brusquement to brake sharply
100 kilomètres à l'heure 100 kilometres an hour
crever, avoir un pneu crevé to have a puncture;
  être à plat to have a flat tyre

ESSENTIAL WORDS (f)
---

une auto, automobile	car
une autoroute	motorway
une autoroute à péage	
🞏	toll motorway
une auto-stoppeuse	
(pl ~s)	hitch-hiker
la caravane	caravan
la carte routière	road map
la déviation 🞏	diversion
la direction 🞏	direction
la distance 🞏	distance
l'eau	water
l'essence 🞏	petrol
l'huile	oil
l'ordinaire	2-star petrol
la police	police
la route	road
la station-service	
(pl ~s~)	service or filling station
la voiture ⟡	car

sais-tu conduire une auto? can you drive a car?
on va faire une promenade en voiture we're going for a drive (in the car)
faites le plein (d'essence)! fill her up please!
l'essence sans plomb unleaded petrol
la route nationale the trunk *or* main road
prenez la route de Lyon take the road to Lyons
perdre/retrouver sa route to lose/find one's way
c'est un voyage de 3 heures it's a 3-hour journey
allez, en route! let's go!, let's be off!
bonne route! have a good journey!
en route nous avons vu . . . on the way we saw . . .
doubler *or* **dépasser une voiture** to overtake a car
garer (la voiture) to park (the car)
je vais faire réparer la voiture I'm going to have the car fixed

---

IMPORTANT WORDS (m)

un accident (de la route)	(road) accident
un automobiliste	motorist
le camionneur	lorry driver
le code de la route 📖	highway code
le coffre ✧	boot
le deux-temps 📖 **(pl inv)**	two-stroke (engine)
le(s) dommage(s)	damage
un embouteillage 📖	traffic jam
l'embrayage 📖	clutch; letting in the clutch
le klaxon	horn, hooter
le lavage 📖	(car) wash
le mort ✧	dead man
le moteur	engine
le motocycliste	motorcyclist
les papiers	official papers, documents
le phare ✧ 📖	headlight; headlamp
le pompiste 📖	petrol pump attendant
le rond-point (pl ~s~s)	roundabout
le sens unique 📖	one-way street
le stationnement 📖	parking

d'abord on met le moteur en marche first you switch on the engine
le moteur démarre the engine starts up
la voiture démarre the car moves off
on roule we're driving along
accélérer to accelerate; **continuer** to continue
ralentir to slow down; **s'arrêter** to stop
stationner to park; to be parked
couper le moteur to switch off the engine
il y a eu un accident there's been an accident
vos papiers, s'il vous plaît your identification please

IMPORTANT WORDS (f)

une amende ⌑	fine
l'assurance ⌑	insurance
une auto-école (pl ~s)	driving school
la batterie ◇	battery
la ceinture de sécurité ⌑	seat belt
la circulation	traffic
la collision	collision
la crevaison	puncture
la frontière	border, frontier
la marque ⌑	make (of car)
la mort ◇	death
la panne	breakdown
la pièce de rechange	spare part
la police d'assurance	insurance policy
la pompiste ⌑	petrol pump attendant
la portière	(car) door
la priorité	priority
la roue	wheel
la roue de secours ⌑	spare wheel
la vitesse ◇	speed; gear
la voiture de dépannage	breakdown van
la zone ⌑	zone, area

aux heures d'affluence at the rush hour, at the peak period
il a eu 100 francs d'amende he got a 100-franc fine
êtes-vous assuré(e)? are you insured?
n'oubliez pas de mettre vos ceintures don't forget to put on your seat belts
à la frontière at the border
être or **tomber en panne** to break down, have a breakdown
je suis tombé(e) en panne sèche I've run out of petrol
la roue avant/arrière the front/back wheel

USEFUL WORDS (m)

un **accélérateur**	accelerator
un **arrêt d'urgence**	emergency stop
le **blessé**	casualty
le **capot**	bonnet
le **carburateur**	carburettor
le **clignotant**	indicator
le **compteur de vitesse**	speedometer
le **conducteur débutant**	learner driver
le **contractuel**	traffic warden
le **démarreur**	starter
le **détour**	detour
un **essuie-glace** (pl inv)	windscreen wiper
le **lave-auto** (pl ~s)	car-wash
le **motard**	motorcycle cop
le **panneau** (pl -x)	road sign
le **parcmètre**	parking meter
le **pare-brise** (pl inv)	windscreen
le **pare-chocs** (pl inv)	bumper
le **périphérique**	ring road
le **poste d'essence**	filling station
le **procès-verbal, P.-V.** (pl ~-**verbaux**)	fine, (parking) ticket
le **rétroviseur**	rear-view or driving mirror
le **routier**	long-distance lorry driver
le **starter**	choke
le **tournant, le virage**	turning, bend
le **volant**	steering wheel

l'accident a fait 6 blessés/morts 6 people were injured/killed in the accident
il faut faire un détour we have to make a detour
une contravention pour excès de vitesse a fine for speeding
dresser un P.-V. contre un conducteur to book a driver

USEFUL WORDS (f)

une agglomération	built-up area
une aire de services	service area
une aire de stationnement	lay-by
la bagnole	(old) car, banger
la bande médiane	central reservation
la boîte de vitesses	gearbox
la bretelle d'accès or **de raccordement**	access road (to motorway)
la caisse ⬦	body, bodywork
la capote	hood
la consommation d'essence	petrol consumption
la contractuelle	traffic warden
la contravention	traffic offence
la dépanneuse	breakdown van
la file (de voitures)	line (of cars), lane
la galerie ⬦	roof rack
la leçon de conduite	driving lesson
la limitation de vitesse	speed limit, speed restriction
la pédale	pedal
la plaque d'immatriculation or **minéralogique**	number plate
la pression ⬦	pressure
la remorque	trailer
la voie ⬦	way, road; lane (on road)
la voie de raccordement	slip road

"priorité à droite" "give way to the right"
"serrez à droite" "keep to the right"
"accès interdit" "no entry"
"stationnement interdit" "no parking"
"travaux" "roadworks"
"passage protégé" *road having priority status*

ESSENTIAL WORDS (m)

un anorak	anorak
le bouton ⇨	button
le chapeau (*pl* **-x**)	hat
le col	collar
le collant	(pair of) tights
le complet	suit
le costume ⇨	suit (*for man*); costume
un imper(méable)	raincoat
le jean ⇨[dʒin], **jeans**	(pair of) jeans
le maillot ⇨ **(de bain)**	swimming costume or trunks
le manteau (*pl* **-x**)	coat
le mouchoir	hankie, handkerchief
le pantalon	(pair of) trousers
le parapluie ⌑	umbrella
le pardessus	overcoat
le pull-over, pull [pyl(ɔvœʀ)]	sweater, jumper, pullover
le pyjama ⌑	(pair of) pyjamas
le sac	bag
le slip de bain	swimming or bathing trunks
le slip ⌑	(under)pants
le soulier	shoe
le T-shirt, tee-shirt	T-shirt, tee-shirt
les vêtements	clothes, clothing

IMPORTANT WORDS (m)

le blouson	bomber jacket
le chemisier	blouse
le gant	glove
le sac à main	handbag
le short [ʃɔʀt]	(pair of) shorts
le tricot ⇨ ⌑	jumper, jersey
un uniforme	uniform
le veston	jacket (*for man*)

ESSENTIAL WORDS (f)

la chaussette	sock
la chaussure	shoe
la chemise	shirt
la chemise de nuit	nightie, nightdress
la cravate	tie
la jupe	skirt
la mode 🕮	fashion
la pointure 🕮	(shoe) size
la robe	dress
la sandale	sandal
la taille ◇	size; waist
la veste	jacket (*for man or woman*)

IMPORTANT WORDS (f)

la botte	boot
la ceinture	belt
la pantoufle	slipper
la poche ◇	pocket

---

le matin je m'habille in the morning I get dressed
le soir je me déshabille in the evening I get undressed
puis je me rhabille then I get dressed again
porter to wear; **mettre** to put on
j'essaie un béret I try on a beret
puis je l'enlève then I take it off
quand je rentre du lycée je me change when I get home from school I get changed
des soldats en uniforme soldiers in uniform
à la mode in fashion
démodé(e) old-fashioned
cela fait très chic that's very smart
cela vous va bien/mal that suits/doesn't suit you
quelle est votre pointure? what (shoe) size do you take?
quelle est votre taille? what size do you take?

USEFUL WORDS (m)

les accessoires	accessories
les bas	stockings
le béret	beret
le bermuda	Bermuda shorts
le(s) bleu(s) de travail	overalls, dungarees
le caleçon	(under)pants
le chandail	(thick) jumper
le chapeau (pl -x)	
melon	bowler hat
le cuissard	cycle pants or shorts
un ensemble pantalon	trouser suit
le foulard	scarf, headsquare
le gilet de corps or	
de peau	vest
le gilet	waistcoat; cardigan
l'habit	evening dress, tails
les haillons: en	
haillons	in rags
les hauts talons	high heels
le jupon	underskirt, petticoat
le képi	(military) cap
le lacet	(shoe)lace
le linge ⇨	washing (*items to be washed*)
le nœud papillon	bow tie
le ruban	ribbon
le sac à bandoulière	shoulder bag
le salon d'essayage	changing room
le soutien-gorge (pl ~s~)	bra, brassiere
le survêtement	track suit
le sweat [swit]	sweatshirt
le tablier	apron
le tailleur ⇨	woman's suit
les talons aiguilles	stiletto heels
les trainings	trainers, training shoes
le tricot de corps	vest

USEFUL WORDS (f)

la blouse	smock, overall
la boutonnière	buttonhole
les bretelles	braces
la cabine d'essayage	changing cubicle
la canne ◇	cane, (walking) stick
la casquette	cap
la création	model (*garment*)
la culotte	pants (*for child*)
une écharpe ◇	scarf
une espadrille	rope-soled sandal, espadrille
la fermeture éclair	zip
la :haute couture	haute couture
la jaquette	woman's jacket
la jupe-culotte (*pl ~s~s*)	culottes
la manche	sleeve
la présentation de mode	fashion show
la robe de chambre	dressing gown
la robe de mariée	wedding dress
la robe du soir	evening dress (*for woman*)
la salopette	dungarees, overalls; (ski) salopettes

long(ue) long; **court(e)** short
une robe à manches courtes/longues a short-sleeved/long-sleeved dress
serré(e) tight; **vague** loose
une jupe serrée/large a tight/full skirt
rayé(e) striped; **à carreaux** checked; **à pois** spotted
une jupe à plis a pleated skirt
les vêtements de détente *or* **de loisir** casual clothes
en tenue de soirée in evening dress

SOME COLOURS	
beige	beige
blanc (blanche)	white
bleu ⇦ (bleue)	blue
brun (brune)	brown
fauve	fawn, tawny
gris (grise)	grey
jaune	yellow
marron ⇦	brown
noir (noire)	black
orange, orangé(e)	orange
pourpre	crimson
rose ⇦	pink
rosé(e)	rosé
rouge	red
vert (verte)	green
violet (violette)	violet, purple
bleu clair	pale blue
bleu foncé	dark blue
bleuâtre, bleuté	bluish
bleu ciel	sky blue
bleu marine	navy blue
bleu roi	royal blue

la couleur colour
de quelle couleur sont tes yeux/tes cheveux?
  what colour are your eyes/is your hair?
vif (vive) colourful, bright
le bleu te va bien blue suits you; the blue one suits
  you
peindre qch en bleu to paint sth blue

SOME COLOURFUL PHRASES

changer de couleur to change colour
la Maison Blanche the White House
un Blanc a white man
une Blanche a white woman
blanc comme la neige as white as snow
Blanche-Neige Snow-White
un steak bleu a very rare steak, an underdone steak
le Petit Chaperon Rouge Little Red Riding Hood
rougir to turn red
rougir de honte/de gêne to blush with shame/with
  embarrassment
pâle comme un linge as white as a sheet
bleu de froid blue with cold
tous les trente-six du mois once in a blue moon
elle brunit she is turning brown
les feuilles roussissent the leaves are turning
  brown
tout(e) bronzé(e) as brown as a berry
il était couvert de bleus he was black and blue
un Noir a black man
une Noire a black woman
un œil poché, un œil au beurre noir a black eye
vert(e) de jalousie green with envy
il a le pouce vert he's got green fingers

ESSENTIAL WORDS (m)

un ordinateur	computer
le programme ▷	program
le programmeur	programmer

IMPORTANT WORDS (m)

le micro-ordinateur	
(pl ~s)	PC, personal computer

USEFUL WORDS (m)

le caractère ▷	character, letter
le clavier	keyboard
le curseur	cursor
le disque dur	hard disk
un écran	monitor, screen
le fichier	file
le jeu électronique	computer game
le lecteur de	
disquettes	disk drive
le listage, listing	print-out
le logiciel	software
le matériel	hardware
le menu	menu
le modem	modem
le moniteur	monitor
le pirateur	
d'informatique	hacker
le progiciel	software package
le software	software
le tableur	spreadsheet (program)

aimer les jeux électroniques to like (playing) computer games

j'ai eu un ordinateur pour mon anniversaire I got a computer for my birthday

portatif(ive) portable

écrire or **rédiger un programme** to write a program

ESSENTIAL WORDS (f)	
la souris	mouse

IMPORTANT WORDS (f)	
la batterie ⇨	battery

USEFUL WORDS (f)	
la base de données	database
la console (de visualisation)	VDU, visual display unit
la disquette	floppy disk
les données	data
la fonction	function
une imprimante	printer
l'informatique ⇨ 🕮	computer science; computer studies
une interface	interface
la machine de traitement de texte	word processor
la manette (de jeu)	joystick
la mémoire	memory
la mémoire morte	ROM, Read-Only Memory
la mémoire vive	RAM, random-access memory
la sauvegarde	back-up
la touche ⇨	key
une unité de disquettes	disk drive unit

introduire *or* **entrer les données** to enter the data
mémoriser les données to store the data
rechercher l'information to retrieve the information

ESSENTIAL WORDS *(m)*

le Canada 📖	Canada
le Danemark 📖	Denmark
les États-Unis	the United States
le Luxembourg 📖	Luxemburg
les Pays-Bas 📖	the Netherlands
le pays de Galles 📖	Wales
le pays ⇨	country

IMPORTANT WORDS *(m)*

le Portugal 📖	Portugal
le Royaume-Uni 📖	United Kingdom

USEFUL WORDS *(m)*

le Brésil	Brazil
le Japon	Japan
le Liban	Lebanon
le Marché commun	the Common Market
le Maroc	Morocco
le Mexique	Mexico
le Pakistan	Pakistan
le Viet-Nam	Vietnam

mon pays natal my native country
la capitale de la France the capital of France
de quel pays venez-vous? what country do you
   come from?
je viens des États-Unis/du Canada/de la France I
   come from the United States/from Canada/from
   France
je suis né(e) en Écosse I was born in Scotland
j'irais aux Pays-Bas/au pays de Galles/en Italie I
   would go to the Netherlands/to Wales/to Italy
je reviens des États-Unis I have just come back
   from the United States
les pays en voie de développement the
   developing countries

ESSENTIAL WORDS (f)

l'**Allemagne** 🕮	Germany
l'**Angleterre**	England
la **Belgique** 🕮	Belgium
l'**Écosse** 🕮	Scotland
l'**Espagne** 🕮	Spain
l'**Europe**	Europe
la **France**	France
la **Grande-Bretagne** 🕮	Great Britain
la **:Hollande** 🕮	Holland
l'**Irlande (du Nord)** 🕮	(Northern) Ireland
l'**Italie** 🕮	Italy
la **Suisse**	Switzerland

USEFUL WORDS (f)

l'**Afrique (du Sud)**	(South) Africa
l'**Algérie**	Algeria
l'**Amérique du Sud**	South America
les **Antilles**	West Indies
l'**Asie**	Asia
l'**Australie**	Australia
l'**Autriche**	Austria
la **Chine**	China
la **Communauté européenne, CE**	European Community, EC
la **Corée (du Nord/du Sud)**	(North/South) Korea
la **Grèce**	Greece
l'**Inde**	India
la **Norvège**	Norway
la **Nouvelle Zélande**	New Zealand
la **Pologne**	Poland
la **Roumanie**	Romania
la **Russie**	Russia
la **Suède**	Sweden
la **Tchécoslovaquie**	Czechoslovakia
la **Tunisie**	Tunisia
l'**U.R.S.S.**	U.S.S.R.

ESSENTIAL WORDS (m)

un **Allemand** 📖	a German
un **Américain**	an American
un **Anglais**	an Englishman
un **Belge** 📖	a Belgian
un **Britannique**	a Briton
un **Canadien** 📖	a Canadian
un **Danois** 📖	a Dane
un **Écossais** 📖	a Scotsman
un **Espagnol** 📖	a Spaniard
un **Européen**	a European
un **Français**	a Frenchman
un **Gallois** 📖	a Welshman
un **:Hollandais** 📖	a Dutchman
un **Irlandais** 📖	an Irishman
un **Italien** 📖	an Italian
un **Luxembourgeois** 📖	a native of Luxemburg
un **Pakistanais**	a Pakistani
un **Portugais** 📖	a Portuguese
un **Suisse**	a Swiss

The forms given here and on the following three pages
are the noun forms (i.e. for people) and begin with a
capital letter:
il est Danois, c'est un Danois he is a Dane
elle est Danoise, c'est une Danoise she is a
   Danish girl *etc*

They can be used as adjectives by converting the
capital into a small letter:
le paysage danois the Danish countryside
une ville danoise a Danish town

un Canadien français a French Canadian
je suis Écossais — je parle anglais I am Scottish —
   I speak English

ESSENTIAL WORDS (f)

une Allemande 🔲	a German (girl *or* woman)
une Américaine	an American (girl *or* woman)
une Anglaise	an Englishwoman, an English girl
une Belge 🔲	a Belgian (girl *or* woman)
une Britannique	a Briton, a British girl *or* woman
une Canadienne	a Canadian (girl *or* woman)
une Danoise 🔲	a Dane, a Danish girl *or* woman
une Écossaise 🔲	a Scotswoman, a Scots girl
une Espagnole 🔲	a Spaniard, a Spanish girl *or* woman
une Européenne	a European
une Française	a Frenchwoman, a French girl
une Galloise 🔲	a Welshwoman, a Welsh girl
une :Hollandaise 🔲	a Dutchwoman, a Dutch girl
une Irlandaise 🔲	an Irishwoman, an Irish girl
une Italienne 🔲	an Italian (girl *or* woman)
une Luxembourgeoise 🔲	a native of Luxemburg
une Pakistanaise	a Pakistani (girl *etc*)
une Portugaise 🔲	a Portuguese (girl *etc*)
une Suisse	a Swiss (girl *or* woman)

une Canadienne française a French Canadian
je suis Écossaise — je parle anglais I am Scottish — I speak English
un étranger (une étrangère) a foreigner, a stranger
travailler/aller à l'étranger to work/go abroad
la nationalité nationality

USEFUL WORDS (m)

un **Africain**	an African
un **Algérien**	an Algerian
un **Antillais**	a West Indian
un **Arabe**	an Arab
un **Asiatique**	an Asian
un **Australien**	an Australian
un **Autrichien**	an Austrian
un **Brésilien**	a Brazilian
un **Chinois**	a Chinese
un **Esquimau**	an Eskimo
un **Finnois, Finlandais**	a Finn
un **Grec**	a Greek
un **Indien**	an Indian
un **Japonais**	a Japanese
un **Marocain**	a Moroccan
un **Mexicain**	a Mexican
un **Néo-Zélandais** (*pl inv*)	a New-Zealander
un **Norvégien**	a Norwegian
un **Peau-Rouge** (*pl ~x~s*)	a Red Indian
un **Polonais**	a Pole
un **Russe**	a Russian
un **Scandinave**	a Scandinavian
un **Suédois**	a Swede
un **Tchèque**	a Czech
un **Tunisien**	a Tunisian
un **Turc**	a Turk
un **Vietnamien**	a Vietnamese
un **Yougoslave**	a Yugoslav

la **religion** religion
un **chrétien** a Christian
un **Juif** a Jew
un **musulman** a Moslem, a Muslim

USEFUL WORDS (f)	
une **Africaine**	an African (girl *or* woman)
une **Algérienne**	an Algerian
une **Antillaise**	a West Indian
une **Arabe**	an Arab
une **Australienne**	an Australian
une **Autrichienne**	an Austrian
une **Brésilienne**	a Brazilian
une **Chinoise**	a Chinese
une **Esquimaude**	an Eskimo
une **Finnoise,**	
Finlandaise	a Finn
une **Grecque**	a Greek
une **Indienne**	an Indian
une **Japonaise**	a Japanese
une **Marocaine**	a Moroccan
une **Mexicaine**	a Mexican
une **Néo-Zélandaise**	
(*pl* ~**s**)	a New-Zealander
une **Norvégienne**	a Norwegian
une **Polonaise**	a Pole
une **Russe**	a Russian
une **Scandinave**	a Scandinavian
une **Suédoise**	a Swede
une **Tchèque**	a Czech
une **Tunisienne**	a Tunisian
une **Turque**	a Turk
une **Vietnamienne**	a Vietnamese
une **Yougoslave**	a Yugoslav

une **chrétienne** a Christian
une **Juive** a Jew, a Jewish girl *or* woman
une **musulmane** a Moslem, a Muslim

ESSENTIAL WORDS (m)	
l'air ⇨	air
un arbre	tree
le bois ⌑	wood
le bruit ⌑	noise
le champ	field
le chasseur ⇨	hunter
le château (pl -x)	castle
le chemin	path, way
le fermier	farmer
l'habitant	inhabitant
le marché	market
le pays ⇨	country; district
le paysan	country man, farmer
le pique-nique ⌑	
(pl ~s)	picnic
le pont ⇨	bridge
le terrain ⇨	soil; ground
le touriste	tourist
le trou	hole
le village	village

en plein air in the open air
je connais le chemin du village I know the way to
the village
ils ont fait tout le chemin à pied/en bicyclette
they walked/cycled the whole way
les gens du pays the local people, the locals
nous avons fait un pique-nique we went for a
picnic
traverser un pont to cross a bridge

ESSENTIAL WORDS (f)

une auberge de
  jeunesse   youth hostel
la barrière ⬦   gate; fence
la camionnette   (small) van
la campagne   country
la canne ⬦   cane, (walking) stick
la ferme   farm, farmhouse
la montagne 📖   mountain
la pierre   stone, rock
la rivière   river
la route   road
la terre   earth, ground
la tour ⬦   tower
la touriste   tourist

à la campagne on trouve . . . in the country you
  find . . .
aller à la campagne to go into the country
habiter la campagne/la ville to live in the country/
  in the town
la rivière/le ruisseau coule the river/the stream
  flows
cultiver la terre to cultivate *or* till the land
se diriger vers to make one's way towards

IMPORTANT WORDS (m)	
un agriculteur	farmer
les campagnards	countryfolk, country people
le fleuve	river
le gendarme (m+f)	gendarme
le lac	lake
le paysage	countryside, scenery
le sommet	top (of hill)

USEFUL WORDS (m)	
le bâton ⇨	stick
le blé	corn; wheat
le buisson	bush
le caillou (pl -x)	pebble
le cottage	cottage
le curé	vicar, priest
un étang	pond
le foin	hay
le fossé	ditch
le :hameau (pl -x)	hamlet
le jonc [ʒɔ̃]	reed
le marais	marsh
le moulin (à vent)	(wind)mill
le piège	trap
le poteau (pl -x) indicateur	signpost
le poteau (pl -x) télégraphique	telegraph pole
le pré	meadow
le ruisseau (pl -x)	stream
le sentier	path

agricole agricultural
paisible, tranquille peaceful
au sommet de la colline at the top of the hill
tomber dans un piège to fall into a trap
s'égarer to get lost, lose one's way

IMPORTANT WORDS (f)

l'agriculture	agriculture
une auberge	inn
la botte (de caoutchouc)	(wellington) boot
la chaussée	roadway
la colline	hill
la feuille	leaf
la forêt	forest
la paysanne	country woman, peasant
la poussière	dust
la propriété	property, estate
la tranquillité	peace
la vallée	valley

USEFUL WORDS (f)

la boue	mud
la bruyère	heather
la carrière ⋄	quarry
la caverne	cave
la chasse	hunting; shooting
la chaumière	(thatched) cottage
la chute d'eau	waterfall
la :haie	hedge
les jumelles ⋄	binoculars
la lande	moor, heath
la mare	pond
la moisson	harvest
la plaine	plain
la récolte	crop, harvest
la rive	bank (of river)
les ruines	ruins
la source	spring, source
la vendange	grape harvest

faire la moisson to bring in the harvest
faire les vendanges to harvest the grapes

ESSENTIAL WORDS (m)
---

l'âge	age
un air ◇	appearance
les cheveux	hair
les yeux	eyes

quel âge avez-vous? how old are you?
j'ai 15 ans, mon frère a 13 ans I'm 15, my brother is 13
il vient d'avoir ses 17 ans he's just (turned) 17
un homme/une femme d'un certain âge a middle-aged man/woman
il/elle a l'air triste he/she looks sad
il/elle a l'air sympa or **sympathique** he/she looks nice or friendly
il/elle a l'air fatigué/fatigué(e) he/she looks tired
de quelle couleur sont tes yeux/tes cheveux? what colour are your eyes/is your hair?
j'ai les cheveux blonds I have blond or fair hair
j'ai les yeux bleus/verts I have blue eyes/green eyes
les cheveux bouclés/ondulés curly/wavy hair
les cheveux bruns dark or brown hair
les cheveux châtains chestnut-coloured hair
les cheveux frisés curly hair
les cheveux roux/noirs/gris red/black/grey hair
les cheveux teints dyed hair
court(e) short; **long(ue)** long
à mon avis in my opinion
joli(e) pretty; **laid(e)** ugly; **affreux(euse)** hideous
beau (and **bel** *before a vowel or aspirate h*) handsome; **belle** beautiful
grand(e) tall; **petit(e)** small
jeune young; **vieux** (and **vieil** *before a vowel or aspirate h*), **vieille** old
gros(se) fat; **mince** slim, thin
maigre skinny, thin
barbu bearded, with a beard; **chauve** bald

ESSENTIAL WORDS (f)

la barbe	beard
la couleur ⌐⌐	colour
la larme	tear
les lunettes	glasses
la moustache	moustache
la personne	person
la pièce d'identité ⌐⌐	(means of) identification
la taille ◇	height, size; waist

il pleurait he was crying; **il souriait** he was smiling
il avait les larmes aux yeux he had tears in his eyes
un homme de taille moyenne a man of average
  height
je mesure or **je fais 1 mètre 70** I am 1 metre 70 tall
agréable/désagréable pleasant/unpleasant
aimable nice
amusant(e) amusing, entertaining
bête stupid
calme/agité(e) calm/excited
célèbre famous
charmant(e) charming
clair(e) fair (of skin), light (of hair, eyes)
content(e)/mécontent(e) pleased/displeased
dégoûtant(e) disgusting
drôle funny
formidable great, fantastic
gai(e)/sérieux(euse) cheerful/serious
gentil(le) kind
heureux(euse) happy; **malheureux(euse)** unhappy,
  unfortunate
important(e) important
méchant(e) naughty
nerveux(euse) nervous, tense
optimiste/pessimiste optimistic/pessimistic
poli polite
sage well-behaved
timide shy

IMPORTANT WORDS (m)

le bouton ⬦	spot, pimple
le caractère ⬦	character, nature
le teint	complexion, colouring
les verres (de contact)	contact lenses

USEFUL WORDS (m)

le défaut	fault; bad quality
le dentier	(set of) false teeth
le géant	giant
le geste	movement, gesture
le grain de beauté	mole, beauty spot
le poids	weight

il a bon caractère he is good-natured or good-tempered

il a mauvais caràctere he is ill-natured or bad-tempered

avoir le teint jaune/pâle to have a sallow/pale complexion

porter des lunettes/des verres de contact to wear glasses/contact lenses

IMPORTANT WORDS (f)	
la beauté	beauty
la confiance	confidence
la conscience	conscience
la curiosité 🔲	curiosity
une expression	expression
l'habitude	habit
l'humeur	mood, humour
la laideur	ugliness
la qualité	(good) quality

USEFUL WORDS (f)	
une allure	walk, gait
la boucle	curl
la cicatrice	scar
la fossette	dimple
la frange	fringe
la :honte	shame
les lentilles	contact lenses
la permanente	perm
la ressemblance	resemblance, similarity
la ride	wrinkle
la sueur	sweat
la tache de rousseur	freckle
la tache de son	freckle
la timidité	shyness, timidity

c'est une bonne personne he or she is a good
person
je suis toujours de bonne humeur I am always in
a good mood
il est de mauvaise humeur he is in a bad mood
il s'est mis en colère he got angry
elle ressemble à sa mère she looks like her mother
il a l'habitude de se ronger les ongles he has a
habit of biting his nails

ESSENTIAL WORDS (m)

l'allemand	German
un ami	friend
l'anglais	English
le camarade (de classe)	(school) friend
le carnet ⟡	notebook
le CES ▢ (*collège d'enseignement secondaire*)	comprehensive school
le club	club
le collège	secondary school
le concert	concert
le copain	pal
les cours	lessons
les cours commerciaux ▢	secretarial studies
le crayon	pencil
le dessin	drawing (*subject, work*)
le devoir	homework exercise
les devoirs	homework
le directeur ⟡	headmaster
le dortoir ▢	dormitory
un échange	exchange
un écolier	schoolboy
un élève	pupil, schoolboy
un emploi du temps ▢	timetable
l'enseignement ▢	education, teaching
l'espagnol	Spanish
un étudiant ▢	student
un examen	exam, examination
le français	French
le groupe	group
l'italien	Italian
le laboratoire ▢	laboratory
le livre ⟡	book
le lycée	secondary school
le magnétophone	tape recorder

ESSENTIAL WORDS (f)

une **amie**	friend
la **biologie**	biology
la **camarade (de classe)**	(school) friend
la **cantine**	dining hall, canteen
la **carte** ◇	map
la **chimie**	chemistry
la **classe** ⌑	class; year; classroom
la **copine**	pal
la **cuisine** ◇	cookery
la **directrice** ◇	headmistress
une **école (primaire)**	primary school
une **écolière**	schoolgirl
l'**éducation physique**	physical education, P.E.
l'**électronique** ⌑	electronics
une **élève**	pupil, schoolgirl
une **erreur**	mistake, error
l'**étude (de)** ⌑	study (of)
les **études** ⌑	studies
une **étudiante** ⌑	student
une **excursion**	trip, outing
une **expérience** ◇ ⌑	experiment
la **faute** ◇ ⌑	mistake
la **géographie**	geography
la **gomme**	rubber
les **grandes vacances**	summer holidays
la **gymnastique**	gym
l'**histoire**	history; story
la **journée**	(whole) day; daytime
les **langues (vivantes)** ◇	(modern) languages
la **leçon (de français)**	(French) lesson
la **lecture**	reading
les **mathématiques, math(s)**	mathematics, maths
la **matière**	(school) subject
la **musique**	music

ESSENTIAL WORDS (m) (cont)

le mot	word
un ordinateur	computer
le prix ⇨	prize
le professeur (m+f)	(secondary school) teacher
le progrès ▭	progress
le résultat	result
le stylo (à encre)	(fountain) pen
le tableau ⇨ (noir)	blackboard
le travail	work
les travaux manuels	handicrafts

travailler to work; **apprendre** to learn; **étudier** to study

aimer to like; **détester** to detest; **préférer** to prefer

depuis combien de temps apprenez-vous le français? how long have you been learning French?

j'apprends le français depuis 3 ans I've been learning French for 3 years

apprendre qch par cœur to learn sth off by heart

j'ai des devoirs tous les soirs I have homework every evening

ma petite sœur va à l'école — moi, je vais au collège my little sister goes to primary school — I go to secondary school

un(e) élève sérieux(euse)/paresseux(euse) a serious/lazy pupil

j'aimerais enseigner le français I would like to teach French

le professeur d'allemand the German teacher

en fin de trimestre j'ai gagné un prix I won a prize at the end of term

j'ai dû faire des progrès I must have made progress

bientôt il me faudra passer un examen soon I'll have to sit an exam

est-ce que je vais être reçu(e) — est-ce que je vais échouer? will I pass — will I fail?

ESSENTIAL WORDS (f) (cont)

la natation 📖	swimming
la note ◇ 📖	mark
la phrase	sentence
la physique	physics
la piscine	swimming pool
la question	question
la récréation	break, interval
la rentrée (des classes)	beginning of term
la réponse	answer, reply
la salle de classe	classroom
la salle des professeurs	staffroom
la science	science
une université 📖	university
les vacances	holidays

facile/difficile easy/difficult
intéressant(e) interesting; **ennuyeux(euse)** boring
lire to read; **écrire** to write; **écouter** to listen (to);
   regarder to look at, watch; **répéter** to repeat;
   répondre to reply; **parler** to speak
elle est (la) première/dernière de la classe she is
   top/bottom of the class
entrer en classe to go into the classroom
**quand je fais une erreur je l'efface et je la
   corrige** when I make a mistake I rub it out and
   correct it
quelquefois nous faisons des excursions
   sometimes we go on trips
j'ai fait une faute de grammaire I made a
   grammatical mistake
ce n'est pas de ma faute it's not my fault
j'ai eu une bonne note I got a good mark or good
   marks
répondez à la question! answer the question!

IMPORTANT WORDS (m)	
un absent	absentee
le baccalauréat, bac ⟡ ⊞	French school-leaving certificate/exam
le brevet ⊞	exam taken at end of 4th form
le bulletin ⊞	report
le bureau ⟡	desk
le certificat	certificate
le classeur	folder, file
le concours ⟡	competitive exam
le couloir ⊞	corridor
le diplôme ⊞	diploma
un instituteur	primary schoolteacher
le jour de congé	day off, holiday
le papier	paper
le règlement	rule

mon ami prépare son bac my friend is sitting his school-leaving exam (*like A-levels*)
les Français ont congé le mercredi French children have Wednesdays off
je vais repasser la leçon demain I'll go over the lesson again tomorrow
repasser ses leçons, réviser to revise

IMPORTANT WORDS (f)

une absence	absence
une absente	absentee
la conférence	lecture
la cour ⇨ **(de récréation)**	playground
une institutrice	primary schoolteacher
la règle	rule; ruler
la traduction	translation (technique, exercise)
la version	(unseen) translation (from French)

en sixième in first year, in the first form
en première in sixth year, in the sixth form
en terminale in final year

You may want to talk about the British concepts of
head boy/head girl and prefects. In French these are:
l'élève (*m/f*) **de terminale chargé(e) d'un certain
   nombre de responsabilités**
and:
l'élève (*m/f*) **des grandes classes chargé(e) de la
   discipline**

présent(e) present; **absent(e)** absent
punir un(e) élève to punish a pupil
mettre une colle à quelqu'un to give somebody
   detention, keep somebody in
taisez-vous! be quiet!

USEFUL WORDS (m)

les arts ménagers	domestic science, homecraft
le bic	ballpoint pen
le brouillon	rough copy
le cahier	exercise book, jotter
le cartable	satchel
le collège technique	technical college
le couvent	convent; convent school
le demi-pensionnaire (pl ~s)	day-boy
le dictionnaire	dictionary
un examinateur	examiner
un exercice	exercise
un externe	day-boy
le feutre	felt-tip pen
le grec	Greek
un internat	boarding school
un interne	boarder
le latin	Latin
le lycéen	secondary school pupil
le pensionnaire ⟡	boarder
le principal	headmaster (of collège)
le proviseur	headmaster (of lycée)
le pupitre	desk
le rang	row (of seats etc)
le russe	Russian
le stylo à bille	ballpoint pen
le stylo feutre	felt-tip pen
le stylomine	propelling pencil
le taille-crayon(s) (pl ~(s))	pencil sharpener
le test	test
le thème	prose translation
le torchon ⟡	duster
le trimestre	term
le vestiaire	cloakroom
le vocabulaire	vocabulary

USEFUL WORDS (f)

l'algèbre	algebra
l'arithmétique	arithmetic
la colle ◇	detention
la composition	composition, essay; class exam
la conduite	behaviour
la couture	sewing, needlework
la craie	chalk
la distribution des prix	prize-giving
une école maternelle	nursery school
une école mixte	mixed school, co-ed
une école normale	College of Education
l'écriture	handwriting
l'encre	ink
une épreuve	test
la faculté, fac	university
la feuille de présence	absence sheet
la géométrie	geometry
la grammaire	grammar
l'informatique ◇ 🕮	computer studies
l'instruction religieuse	religious instruction
une interne	boarder
la lycéenne	secondary school pupil
la machine à calculer	calculator
la menuiserie	woodwork
la moyenne	fifty per cent, half marks
l'orthographe	spelling
la poésie	poetry
la punition	punishment
la retenue	detention
la sacoche ◇	schoolbag, satchel
les sciences naturelles	biology, natural history
la serviette ◇	briefcase
la tache	blot
la tâche	task

ESSENTIAL WORDS (m)

l'air ⟡	air
les Amis de la Terre	Friends of the Earth
les animaux	animals
les arbres	trees
le bois ⌑	wood
un écologiste	environmentalist, ecologist
l'environnement ⌑	environment
les fruits	fruit
le gas-oil ⌑	diesel
le gaz	gas
les habitants	inhabitants
le journal (*pl* journaux)	newspaper
les légumes	vegetables
le magazine	magazine
le monde ⌑	world
le pays ⟡	country
les poissons	fish
le temps ⟡	weather; time
le trou	hole
les Verts	the Greens
le verre	glass

IMPORTANT WORDS (m)

l'aluminium	aluminium
un article	article
l'avenir	future
le climat ⌑	climate
le déodorant	deodorant
le détergent	detergent
le(s) dommage(s)	damage
un événement	event
le fleuve	river
le gouvernement	government
le lac	lake
le polluant ⌑	pollutant

ESSENTIAL WORDS (f)

les autos	cars
les bouteilles	bottles
la carte ⇨	map
la côte ⇨	coast
l'eau	water
l'essence ⌂	petrol
les fleurs	flowers
une île	island
les informations ⌂	news
la mer	sea
la montagne ⌂	mountain
la plage	beach
les plantes	plants
la pluie	rain
la pollution ⌂	pollution
la question	question
la région	region, area
la rivière	river
la température	temperature
la terre	earth
une usine	factory

IMPORTANT WORDS (f)

la chaleur	heat
la crise	crisis
la forêt	forest
la lessive	washing powder; washing
la nourriture	food
la planète	planet
la solution	solution
la taxe ⌂	tax
la zone ⌂	zone

USEFUL WORDS (m)

un atomiseur   aerosol
le canal (pl canaux)   canal
le chercheur   researcher
les chlorofluoro-
   carbures (CFC)   chlorofluorocarbons (CFC)
le combustible   fuel
le continent   continent
les déchets nucléaires/
   industriels   nuclear/industrial waste
le dépotoir   dumping ground
le désert   desert
un engrais (chimique)   (artificial) fertilizer
un océan   ocean
le pot catalytique   catalytic converter
le produit   product
les produits chimiques   chemicals
le réchauffement de
   la terre   global warming
les scientifiques   scientists
l'univers   universe

j'aimerais faire le tour du monde I'd like to go
round the world
le meilleur (la meilleure) du monde the best in the
world
il y a beaucoup de monde there are lots of people
à l'avenir in the future

USEFUL WORDS (f)

la catastrophe	catastrophe
la couche d'ozone	ozone layer
la forêt tropicale humide	tropical rainforest
la lune	moon
la nocivité	harmfulness
les pluies acides	acid rain
la population	population
les vidanges	sewage

polluer to pollute
détrulre to destroy
contaminer to contaminate
interdire qch to ban sth
sauver to save
recycler to recycle
vert(e) green
biodégradable biodegradable
nocif(ive) pour l'environnement harmful to the environment
bon(ne) pour la nature environment-friendly
organique organic
l'essence sans plomb unleaded petrol

ESSENTIAL WORDS (m)

les adultes	adults
l'âge	age
le bébé 🔲	baby
le cousin 🔲	cousin
un enfant 🔲	child
le fiancé	fiancé
le fils [fis]	son
le frère	brother
le garçon ⇨	boy
les gens 🔲	people
le grand-père	
(*pl* ~s~s)	grandfather
les grands-parents	grandparents
l'homme	man
le jeune homme	youth, young man
le mari 🔲	husband
le nom	name
le nom de famille	surname
un oncle	uncle
le parent	parent; relation, relative
les parents	parents; relations, relatives
le père	father
le prénom	first *or* Christian name

quel âge avez-vous? how old are you?
j'ai 15 ans — il a 40 ans I'm 15 — he is 40
comment vous appelez-vous? what is your name?
je m'appelle Robert my name is Robert
il s'appelle Jean-Pierre his name is Jean-Pierre
fiancé(e) engaged; **marié(e)** married; **divorcé(e)**
   divorced; **séparé(e)** separated
épouser qn, se marier avec qn to marry sb
se marier to get married; **divorcer** to get divorced
**quel est votre nom/votre nom de famille/votre
   prénom?** what is your name/your surname/your
   first name?
nom de jeune fille maiden name

ESSENTIAL WORDS (f)

la cousine 🕮	cousin
la dame ◊	lady
une enfant	child
la famille	family
la femme	woman; wife
la fiancée	fiancée
la fille	daughter
les gens 🕮	people
la grand-mère	
(*pl* ~(**s**)~**s**)	grandmother
les grandes personnes	grown-ups
la jeune fille	girl
la mère	mother
la personne	person; (*in plural*) people
la sœur	sister
la tante	aunt

maman! mummy!; **papa!** daddy!

j'ai un frère et une sœur I have one brother and one sister

plus âgé(e) que moi older than me

plus jeune que moi younger than me

je n'ai pas de frères/de sœurs I don't have any brothers/sisters

je suis enfant unique I am an only child

toute la famille the whole family

grandir to grow; **vieillir** to get old

les jeunes, les jeunes gens young people

je m'entends bien avec mes parents I get on well with my parents

compréhensif(ive) understanding

j'ai des disputes avec ma sœur I have arguments with my sister

ma mère travaille au dehors my mother goes out to work

la nurse s'occupe des enfants the nanny looks after the children

---

IMPORTANT WORDS (m)

un adolescent	teenager
l'aîné	elder, eldest
le beau-père	
(pl ~x~s)	father-in-law; stepfather
le cadet	younger, youngest
le célibataire	bachelor
l'époux	husband, spouse
le neveu	nephew
le petit-fils [pətifis]	
(pl ~s~)	grandson
les petits-enfants	
[pətizɑ̃fɑ̃]	grandchildren
le veuf	widower
le voisin	neighbour

USEFUL WORDS (m)

le beau-fils [bofis]	
(pl ~x~s)	son-in-law
le beau-frère (pl ~x~s)	brother-in-law
le couple	couple
le demi-frère (pl ~s)	stepbrother
le gendre	son-in-law
le gosse	kid
les jumeaux	twins
le marié	bridegroom
les nouveaux mariés	newly-weds
un orphelin	orphan
le parrain	godfather
le retraité	(old age) pensioner
le surnom	nickname
les triplés	triplets
le vieillard	old man

---

naître to be born; **vivre** to live; **mourir** to die
je suis né(e) en 1980 I was born in 1980
ma grand-mère est morte my grandmother is dead
elle est morte en 1985 she died in 1985

IMPORTANT WORDS (f)

une **adolescente**	teenager
l'**aînée**	elder, eldest
l'**allocation familiale**	
&#x1F4D6;	child benefit
la **belle-mère**	mother-in-law;
(pl ~s~s)	stepmother
la **cadette**	younger, youngest
la **célibataire**	spinster
une **épouse**	wife, spouse
la **jeune fille au pair**	au pair girl
la **jeunesse**	youth (of life); young people
la **nièce**	niece
la **petite-fille** (pl ~s~s)	granddaughter
la **veuve**	widow
la **voisine**	neighbour

USEFUL WORDS (f)

la **belle-fille** (pl ~s~s)	daughter-in-law
la **belle-sœur** (pl ~s~s)	sister-in-law
la **demi-sœur** (pl ~s)	stepsister
la **femme au foyer**	housewife
la **gosse**	kid
la **jeune mariée**	bride
les **jumelles** ⇒	twins, twin sisters
la **marraine**	godmother
la **ménagère**	housewife
la **nurse**	nanny
une **orpheline**	orphan
la **retraitée**	(old age) pensioner
la **vieillesse**	old age

il/elle est célibataire he/she is not married, he is a bachelor/she is a spinster

il est veuf he is a widower; **elle est veuve** she is a widow

un(e) des voisins one of the neighbours

ESSENTIAL WORDS (m)

un animal (*pl* **animaux**)	animal
le bœuf ◇ [bœef]	
(*pl* **-s** [bø])	ox
le canard	duck
le champ	field
le chat	cat
le cheval (*pl* **chevaux**)	horse
le chien	dog
le cochon	pig
le dindon	turkey
le fermier	farmer
le mouton ◇	sheep
le pays ◇	country; district
le poulet	chicken
le tas	heap, pile
le veau ◇ (*pl* **-x**)	calf
le village	village

IMPORTANT WORDS (m)

un agneau (*pl* **-x**)	lamb
le coq	cock
le paysan	country person, peasant
le tracteur	tractor

un champ de blé a field of corn
cultiver les champs to plough the fields
le chien de berger the sheepdog

ESSENTIAL WORDS (f)

la barrière ▷	gate; fence
la camionnette	(small) van
la campagne	country
la ferme	farm, farmhouse
la fermière	farmer's wife
la forêt	forest
la poule ▭	hen
la terre	earth, ground
la vache	cow

IMPORTANT WORDS (f)

la colline	hill
la paysanne	country woman, peasant
la poussière	dust

vivre à la campagne to live in the country
travailler dans une ferme to work on a farm
la ferme est située au milieu d'un champ the
   farm is in the middle of a field

USEFUL WORDS (m)	
un âne	donkey
le bélier	ram
le berger	shepherd
le bétail	cattle
le blé	corn; wheat
le chevreau (pl -x)	kid
un épouvantail	scarecrow
un étang	pond
le foin	hay
le fossé	ditch
le fumier	manure
le grain	grain, seed
le grenier ⇨	loft
le :hangar	shed, barn
le laboureur	ploughman
le maïs [ma-is]	maize
le moulin (à vent)	(wind)mill
le porc ⇨ [pɔʀ]	pig
le poulailler ⇨	henhouse, hen coop
le poulain	foal
le poussin	chick, chicken
le pré	meadow
le puits	well
le ruisseau (pl -x)	stream
le seau (pl -x)	bucket, pail
le seigle	rye
le sillon	furrow
le sol	ground, earth, land
le taureau (pl -x)	bull
le troupeau (pl -x)	(*sheep*) flock; (*cattle*) herd

s'occuper des animaux to look after the animals
ils mangent du foin et boivent de l'eau they eat hay and drink water

USEFUL WORDS (f)

l'avoine	oats
la baratte	churn
la basse-cour (pl ~s~s)	farmyard
la boue	mud
la céréale	cereal crop
la charrette	cart
la charrue	plough
la chaumière	(thatched) cottage
la chèvre	goat
une échelle	ladder
une écurie	stable
une étable	cow-shed, byre
la fièvre aphteuse	foot and mouth disease
la gerbe	sheaf
la grange	barn
la lande	moor, heath
la meule de foin	haystack
la moisson	harvest
la moissoneuse-batteuse (pl ~s~s)	combine harvester
une oie	goose
l'orge	barley
la paille ⬦	straw
la palissade	fence
la porcherie	pigsty
la récolte	crop
la vigne	vine

rentrer la moisson to bring in the harvest
faire la récolte to bring in the crops

ESSENTIAL WORDS (m)

l'air ⇨	air
les fruits de mer 📖	shellfish, seafood
le poisson	fish
le poisson rouge	goldfish

IMPORTANT WORDS (m)

le crabe	crab
un insecte	insect

USEFUL WORDS (m)

le brochet	pike
le cafard	beetle
le calmar	squid
le criquet	cricket
le frelon	hornet
le grillon	cricket
le :haddock	haddock
le :hareng	herring
le :homard	lobster
le merlan	whiting
le moucheron	midge
le moustique	mosquito
le papillon	butterfly
le papillon de nuit	moth
le phasme	stick insect
le poulpe	octopus
le requin	shark
le saumon	salmon
le têtard	tadpole
le thon	tuna
le ver	worm
le ver à soie	silkworm

---

nager dans l'eau to swim in the water
voler dans l'air to fly in the air
nous allons à la pêche we're going fishing

ESSENTIAL WORDS (f)

l'eau   water

IMPORTANT WORDS (f)

la mouche   fly
la queue ▷ [kø]   tail
la sardine   sardine
la truite   trout

USEFUL WORDS (f)

une abeille   bee
une aile   wing
une anguille   eel
une araignée   spider
la bête à bon dieu   ladybird
la chenille   caterpillar
la cigale   cicada
la coccinelle [kɔksinɛl]   ladybird
la crevette   shrimp
la fourmi   ant
la grenouille   frog
la guêpe   wasp
l'huître   oyster
la langouste   crawfish, crayfish
les langoustines   scampi
la libellule   dragonfly
la méduse   jellyfish
la morue   cod
la mouche à vers   bluebottle
la moule   mussel
la pieuvre   octopus
la puce   flea
la punaise ▷   bug
la sauterelle   grasshopper
la sole   sole

---

l'abeille/la guêpe pique the bee/the wasp stings
une toile d'araignée a spider's web

ESSENTIAL WORDS (m)	
un apéritif 🕮	aperitif
le bar 🕮	bar
le beurre	butter
le bifteck 🕮	steak
le biscuit	biscuit
le bœuf ◇	beef
le bol	bowl
les bonbons	sweets
le café ◇	coffee; café
le chocolat (chaud)	(hot) chocolate
le cidre 🕮	cider
le coca	Coke, coca cola
le couteau (pl -x)	knife
le croissant	croissant
le croque-monsieur	toasted sandwich
(pl inv)	(ham/cheese)
le déjeuner	lunch
le demi	a half (bottle/litre etc)
le dessert	dessert
le dîner	dinner
le fromage	cheese
un fruit	a piece of fruit, some fruit
les fruits	fruit
les fruits de mer 🕮	seafood, shellfish
le garçon ◇	waiter
le gâteau (pl -x)	cake
le :hamburger	beefburger
les :hors-d'œuvre 🕮	hors d'œuvres, starters
le jambon	ham
le jus de fruit	fruit juice
le lait	milk
les légumes	vegetables
le menu	(fixed-price) menu
un œuf [œf] (pl -s [ø])	egg
le pain	bread; loaf
le pain grillé	toast
le pain au chocolat	chocolate croissant

ESSENTIAL WORDS (f)	
l'addition	bill
une assiette	plate
la baguette	French loaf
la bière	beer
la boisson	drink
la boîte	tin, can; box
la bouteille	bottle
la carte ◇	menu
la confiture	jam
la confiture d'oranges	marmalade
la crêpe ▢	pancake
les crudités ▢	selection of salads
la cuiller, cuillère	spoon
l'eau (minérale)	(mineral) water
une entrée ◇ ▢	first course
la faim	hunger
la fourchette	fork
les frites	chips, French fries
la glace ◇	ice cream
l'huile	oil
la limonade	lemonade
une olive	olive
une omelette	omelette
la pâtisserie ◇ ▢	pastry; pastries
les pommes frites	chips
la quiche	quiche
la salade	salad
la saucisse	sausage
la soif	thirst
la soucoupe	saucer
la soupe	soup
la table	table
la tasse	cup
la tranche (de) ▢	slice (of)
la vaisselle	dishes
la viande	meat

ESSENTIAL WORDS *(m) (cont)*	
le pâté	pâté
le patron ⋄	owner
le petit déjeuner	breakfast
le pique-nique (*pl* ~s) 🔲	picnic
le plat	dish; course
le plateau ⋄ (*pl* -x)	tray
les plats cuisinés 🔲	cooked dishes
le poisson	fish
le porc ⋄ [pɔʀ]	pork
le potage	soup
le poulet (rôti)	(roast) chicken
le quart	a quarter (*bottle/litre etc*)
le repas	meal
le restaurant	restaurant
le riz	rice
le rôti 🔲	roast
le sandwich [sɑ̃dwitʃ]	sandwich
le saucisson	(*large*) slicing sausage
le sel	salt
le service	service
le souper	supper
le steak [stɛk]	steak
le sucre	sugar
le thé	tea
le veau ⋄ 🔲	veal
le verre	glass
le vin	wine
le vinaigre	vinegar
le yaourt	yoghurt

manger to eat; **boire** to drink; **avaler** to swallow
j'aime beaucoup I like; **je déteste** I hate; **je préfère** I prefer
mon repas préféré my favourite meal
qu'est-ce que tu prends à boire? what are you having to drink?

SMOKING

ESSENTIAL WORDS (m)
---

le briquet	lighter
le tabac ⋄	tobacco; tobacconist's

IMPORTANT WORDS (m)
---

le cendrier	ashtray
le cigare	cigar

ESSENTIAL WORDS (f)
---

une allumette	match
la cigarette	cigarette

IMPORTANT WORDS (f)
---

la pipe	pipe

une boîte d'allumettes a box of matches
avez-vous du feu? do you have a light?
allumer une cigarette to light (up) a cigarette
"défense de fumer" "no smoking"
je ne fume pas I don't smoke
j'ai arrêté de fumer I've stopped smoking

IMPORTANT WORDS (m)	
l'agneau	lamb (*meat*)
le chariot	(supermarket) trolley
le chef ⇨ (de cuisine) (*m+f*)	chef, head cook
le choix ☐	choice
le couvert ☐	cover charge; place setting
les escargots	snails
le goût ☐	taste
le goûter	tea (*meal*)
le lapin ☐	rabbit
le mouton ⇨	mutton
un Orangina	fizzy drink with orange pulp
le parfum ⇨ ☐	flavour
le pichet ☐	jug
le poivre	pepper
le pourboire ☐	tip
le prix net ☐	inclusive price
les salés ☐	savouries
le serveur	waiter
le sirop	syrup; concentrate
les sucrés ☐	sweet things
le supplément ☐	extra charge

c'est bon/pas bon it's nice/not nice
déjeuner to have lunch; **dîner** to have dinner; **goûter** to taste
ça sent bon! that smells good!
le vin blanc/rosé/rouge white/rosé/red wine
avoir faim to be hungry; **avoir soif** to be thirsty
j'ai faim et j'ai soif I'm hungry and thirsty
mettre le couvert, mettre la table to set *or* lay the table
débarrasser to clear the table
faire la vaisselle to do the dishes *or* the washing-up

IMPORTANT WORDS (f)

la carafe	carafe, jug
les chips	crisps
la côte ◇	chop
la crème ◇	cream
la cuiller à café/à dessert/de service	teaspoon/dessert spoon/tablespoon
la farine	flour
la mayonnaise ▭	mayonnaise
la moutarde	mustard
l'odeur	smell
la pizza	pizza
la pression ◇ ▭	draught beer
la recette	recipe
la serveuse	waitress
la tarte	tart
la terrine ▭	terrine, pâté
la théière	teapot

délicieux(ieuse) delicious
appétissant(e) appetizing
dégoûtant(e) disgusting
"plat du jour" "dish of the day"
"spécialité de la maison" "speciality of the house"
bon appétit! enjoy your meal!
à votre santé! good health!, cheers!
l'addition s'il vous plaît! the bill please!
est-ce que le service est compris? is service included?
"service (non) compris" "service (not) included"

USEFUL WORDS (*m*)	
le **bouchon**	cork
le **cacao**	cocoa
le **casse-croûte** (*pl inv*)	snack
le **champagne**	champagne
le **citron pressé**	fresh lemon drink
le **cognac**	brandy
le **diplomate**	
(à l'anglaise)	trifle
le **foie**	liver
le **gibier**	game
le **glaçon** ⋄	ice cube
le **:haggis**	haggis
le **ketchup**	tomato ketchup
le **lard**	bacon
les **lardons**	(chopped) bacon
le **miel**	honey
le **panaché**	shandy
le **petit pain**	roll
le **pot à lait**	milk jug
le **ragoût**	stew
les **rognons**	kidneys
le **rosbif**	roast beef
le **thermos**	flask
un **toast**	slice *or* piece of toast
le **whisky**	whisky

USEFUL WORDS (f)	

une assiette anglaise	selection of cold meats
la biscotte	toast (*in packets*)
la brioche	bun
la carte des vins	wine-list
la côtelette	chop
la crème anglaise	custard
la crème Chantilly	whipped cream
la cruche	(milk) jug
les cuisses de grenouille	frogs' legs
la gelée ▷	jelly
une infusion	herb(al) tea
la margarine	margarine
la miette	crumb
les moules	mussels
la nappe	table cloth
la nourriture	food
la paille ▷	(*drinking*) straw
les pâtes	pasta
la purée	mashed potatoes
les rillettes	potted meat (*made of pork or goose*)
la sauce	sauce; gravy
la sauce vinaigrette	vinaigrette sauce
la serviette ▷	napkin, serviette
la tartine (de beurre)	piece of bread and butter
la tisane	herb(al) tea
les tripes	tripe
la volaille	poultry

ESSENTIAL WORDS (m)

un **appareil(-photo)** (pl ~s~s)	camera
l'**argent de poche**	pocket money
le **baby-sitting**	baby-sitting
le **babyfoot**	table football
le **bal**	dance
le **billet** ⇨	ticket
le **chanteur (pop)**	(pop) singer
le **cinéma**	cinema
le **club (des jeunes)**	(youth) club
le **concert**	concert
le **correspondant**	pen friend
le **disque**	record
les **échecs**	chess
un **électrophone**	record player
le **film**	film
le **jeu** ⇨ (pl -x)	game; acting; gambling
le **journal** (pl journaux)	newspaper
le **magazine**	magazine
le **magnétophone (à cassettes)**	(cassette) recorder
le **membre**	member
le **musée**	museum; art gallery
le **passe-temps** (pl inv)	hobby
le **programme** ⇨	(TV) programme
le **roman**	novel
le **spectacle**	show
le **temps libre**	free time, spare time
le **théâtre**	theatre
le **transistor**	transistor
le **week-end** (pl ~s)	weekend; at the weekend

comment passez-vous le temps? what do you do to pass the time?

je m'intéresse à la musique/aux sports I am interested in music/sport

je sors avec mes amis I go out with my friends

ESSENTIAL WORDS (f)	
la boum	party
la brochure	leaflet
les cartes ⇨	cards
la cassette	cassette
la chanson	singing; song
la chanteuse (pop)	(pop) singer
la correspondante	pen friend
la disco(thèque) ⇨	disco
la distraction	hobby, entertainment
une excursion	trip, outing
les informations ⌑	news
la lecture	reading
la musique (pop/ classique)	(pop/classical) music
la photo	photo
la promenade ⇨	walk; trip, outing
la publicité ⌑	publicity
la radio	radio
la revue ⌑	magazine
la surprise-partie (pl ~s~s)	party
la télé(vision)	tv, television
la vedette ⇨ (de cinéma) (m+f)	(film) star

je lis les journaux, je regarde la télévision I read
  the newspapers, I watch television
mon hobby préféré my favourite hobby
je m'amuse à bricoler/à faire du baby-sitting I
  enjoy doing odd jobs/baby-sitting
je joue au football/au tennis/aux cartes I play
  football/tennis/cards
je joue du piano/de la guitare *etc* I play the
  piano/guitar *etc*
où on se rencontre? where shall we meet?
je passerai chez toi I'll call round for you

IMPORTANT WORDS (m)

le concours ⇨	competition
le dessin animé	cartoon
le disque compact ⌑	compact disc, CD
le feuilleton	serial; series; "soap"
le :hobby ⌑	hobby
un intérêt	interest
le jouet ⌑	toy
les loisirs	leisure (activities)
le magnétoscope	video (recorder)
le micro-ordinateur (pl ~s)	PC, personal computer
le petit ami	boyfriend
le son et lumière ⌑	sound and light show
le télé-journal	TV news
le tricot ⇨	knitting

USEFUL WORDS (m)

le 33 tours	LP
le 45 tours	single (record)
un appareil à sous	one-armed bandit, slot machine
un éclaireur	scout
le fan [fan]	fan
le :hit-parade	charts, hit parade
les mots croisés	crossword puzzle(s)
le palmarès	hit parade
le scout	scout
le vidéoclub	video shop
le Walkman ®	personal stereo

---

passionnant(e) exciting; **ennuyeux(euse)** boring
amusant(e) funny; **pas mal** not bad, quite good
faire des photos to take photos
si je m'ennuie je . . . if I get bored I . . .

IMPORTANT WORDS (f)

les actualités	news
une affiche	notice; poster
la bande ◇	(recording) tape
la collection	collection
une émission	(TV) programme
une exposition	exhibition, show
la maison des jeunes	youth club
la peinture ◇	painting (*subject, work*)
la pellicule	film (*for camera*)
la petite amie	girlfriend
la (petite) annonce	advert; small ad
la randonnée ▭	walk; hike; drive
la réunion	meeting
la soirée	evening
la tapisserie ◇	tapestry
la vidéocassette	video (cassette)

USEFUL WORDS (f)

la boîte de nuit	night club
la chorale	choir
la colonie de vacances	holiday camp
la couture	sewing, needlework
les dames ◇	draughts
la diapositive	slide, transparency
une éclaireuse	girl guide
la grosse radio-cassette	ghetto-blaster
la photographie	photograph; photography
la planche à roulettes	skateboard

---

on se réunit le vendredi we meet on Fridays
gagner to earn; **emprunter** to borrow; **prêter** to
   lend; **coûter** to cost; **payer** to pay; **acheter** to
   buy; **rembourser** to pay back
à court d'argent short of money
je fais des économies pour acheter un Walkman
   I'm saving up to buy a Walkman

ESSENTIAL WORDS (m)

un abricot	apricot
un ananas	pineapple
le citron	lemon
un fruit	a piece of fruit, some fruit
les fruits	fruit
le marron ⟡ (grillé)	(roasted) chestnut
le pamplemousse	grapefruit
le raisin	grape(s)

IMPORTANT WORDS (m)

un abricotier	apricot tree
un arbre fruitier	fruit tree
le bananier	banana tree
le cerisier	cherry tree
le citronnier	lemon tree
le melon	melon
l'oranger	orange tree
le pêcher	peach tree
le poirier	pear tree
le pommier	apple tree

USEFUL WORDS (m)

un avocat ⟡	avocado pear
le cassis	blackcurrant (fruit, bush)
le dattier	date palm
le figuier	fig tree
le fruit de la passion	passion fruit
le kiwi	kiwi-fruit
le noisetier	hazel tree
le noyau (pl -x)	stone (in fruit)
le noyer	walnut tree
le pépin	pip (in fruit)
le pruneau (pl -x)	prune
le prunier	plum tree
le verger	orchard
le vignoble	vineyard

ESSENTIAL WORDS (f)	
la banane	banana
la cerise	cherry
la fraise	strawberry
la framboise	raspberry
une orange	orange
la pêche ◇	peach
la poire	pear
la pomme	apple
la tomate	tomato; tomato plant

IMPORTANT WORDS (f)	
la peau ▭	skin

USEFUL WORDS (f)	
la baie ◇	berry
la datte	date
la figue	fig
la grenade	pomegranate
la groseille	redcurrant
la groseille à	
maquereau	gooseberry
la mandarine	tangerine
la mûre	blackberry, bramble
la myrtille	bilberry
la noisette	hazelnut
la noix	nut; walnut
la noix de coco	coconut
la prune	plum
la rhubarbe	rhubarb
la vigne	vine

un jus d'orange/d'ananas an orange/a pineapple
juice
une grappe de raisin a bunch of grapes
les raisins secs raisins
mûr(e) ripe; **pas mûr(e)** unripe

ESSENTIAL WORDS (m)

le **congélateur**	freezer
un **électrophone**	record player
le **fauteuil**	armchair
le **frigidaire, frigo**	fridge
le **lit**	bed
un **meuble** 🖪	a piece of furniture
les **meubles** 🖪	furniture
le **miroir**	mirror
le **placard**	cupboard
le **radiateur** 🖪	radiator, heater
le **rayon** ◇	shelf
le **téléphone**	telephone
le **téléviseur (couleur)**	(colour) television
le **transistor**	transistor (radio)

IMPORTANT WORDS (m)

un **appareil**	appliance; device
un **aspirateur**	vacuum cleaner, Hoover®
le **buffet** ◇	sideboard
le **bureau** ◇ (pl -x)	bureau, writing desk
le **canapé**	sofa, settee, couch
le **coffre** ◇	chest
le **lecteur de disque compact** 🖪	CD player
le **magnétophone**	tape recorder
le **magnétoscope**	video (recorder)
le **piano** 🖪	piano
le **tableau** (pl -x)	picture

un **appartement meublé/une pièce meublée** a
furnished flat/room

allumer/éteindre le radiateur to switch on/off the
heater

je fais mon lit le matin I make my bed in the
morning

s'asseoir to sit down; **asseyez-vous!** (do) sit down!

ESSENTIAL WORDS (f)

une armoire	wardrobe
la chaîne stéréo	stereo system
la chaise	chair, seat
la cuisinière ⟡ ▭	
(électrique/à gaz)	(electric/gas) cooker
la glace ⟡	mirror
la lampe	lamp
la machine à laver ▭	washing machine
la maison	house
la pendule	clock
la pièce ⟡	room
la radio	radio
la table	table
la télévision	television

IMPORTANT WORDS (f)

la bibliothèque ⟡	bookcase
la peinture ⟡	painting
la table basse	coffee table

c'est un appartement de 4 pièces it's a 4-roomed flat

mettre le couvert, mettre la table to set *or* lay the table

à table, tout le monde! come and eat, everybody!, dinner (*or lunch etc*) is ready!

j'ai vu à la télévision . . . I saw on television . . .

j'ai entendu à la radio . . . I heard on the radio . . .

USEFUL WORDS (m)

le berceau (pl **-x**)	cradle
le cadre ◇	frame
le camion de déménagement	removal van
le déménagement	removal
le déménageur	removal man
le four	oven
le lampadaire	standard lamp
le lit d'enfant	cot
les lits superposés	bunk beds
le matelas	mattress
le mobilier	furniture
le porte-parapluies (pl inv)	umbrella stand
le répondeur automatique	telephone answering machine
le sèche-cheveux (pl inv)	hair-dryer
le secrétaire ◇	writing desk
le siège	seat
le store	blind
le tabouret	stool
le téléphone sans fil	cordless telephone
le tiroir	drawer
le tourne-disque (pl ~**s**)	record player

mettre qch au four to put sth in the oven
les stores vénitiens Venetian blinds

USEFUL WORDS (f)

la caméra	cine camera
la caméra vidéo	video camera, camcorder
la chaîne compacte (stéréo)	music centre
la coiffeuse ⇨	dressing table
la commode	chest of drawers
une étagère	(set of) shelves
la moquette	fitted carpet
la table de chevet	bedside table
la table de toilette	dressing table
la table roulante	trolley

une machine à coudre/à tricoter a sewing/knitting machine
une machine à écrire a typewriter
une pendule à coucou a cuckoo clock
une table à repasser an ironing board or table

ESSENTIAL WORDS

les Alpes (*fpl*)	the Alps
l'Atlantique (*m*)	the Atlantic
Bordeaux	Bordeaux
Boulogne	Boulogne
la Bourgogne	Burgundy
la Bretagne	Brittany
Bruxelles	Brussels
Calais	Calais
la Côte d'Azur	the Cote d'Azur
Dieppe	Dieppe
Douvres	Dover
Édimbourg	Edinburgh
la Garonne	the Garonne
le :Havre	le Havre
la Loire	the Loire
Londres	London
Lyon	Lyons
la Manche	the English Channel
Marseille	Marseilles
le Massif Central	the Massif Central
la (mer) Méditerranée	the Mediterranean
la mer du Nord	the North Sea
le Midi	the Midi, the South of France
la Normandie	Normandy
Paris	Paris
les Pyrénées (*fpl*)	the Pyrenees
le Rhône	the Rhone
la Seine	the Seine
Strasbourg	Strasbourg, Strasburg

IMPORTANT WORDS

la Dordogne 📖	the Dordogne
Québec 📖	Quebec (city)
le Québec 📖	Quebec (state)
le Rhin 📖	the Rhine
la Tamise 📖	the Thames

USEFUL WORDS	
Alger	Algiers
Anvers	Antwerp
Athènes	Athens
Bâle	Basle
Barcelone	Barcelona
Berlin	Berlin
le Caire	Cairo
la Corse	Corsica
l'Extrême-Orient (*m*)	the Far East
Genève	Geneva
la Haye	The Hague
les îles (*fpl*) **anglo-**	
normandes	the Channel Islands
les îles Britanniques	the British Isles
le Jura	the Jura Mountains
le lac Léman	Lake Geneva
Lisbonne	Lisbon
Moscou	Moscow
le Moyen-Orient	the Middle East
le Pacifique	the Pacific
Pékin	Beijing
le Pôle nord/sud	the North/South Pole
le Proche-Orient	the Near East
la Sardaigne	Sardinia
Varsovie	Warsaw
Venise	Venice
Vienne (*Autriche*)	Vienna
les Vosges (*fpl*)	the Vosges Mountains

aujourd'hui je vais à Calais/au Havre today I'm
   going to Calais/to Le Havre
je viens de Londres/du Massif Central I come
   from London/from the Massif Central
je vais en Normandie I'm going to Normandy
la capitale the capital; **le chef-lieu** the main town

GREETINGS

bonjour hello; good morning; good afternoon
salut hello, hi; goodbye
ça va? how are you?, how's things?
ça va! (*in reply*) fine!
enchanté(e) (very) pleased to meet you
allô hello (*on telephone*)
bonsoir good evening, hello; good night
bonne nuit good night (*when going to bed*)
au revoir goodbye
à demain see you tomorrow
à bientôt, à tout à l'heure see you later
adieu goodbye, farewell

BEST WISHES

bon anniversaire happy birthday
bonne fête happy "saint's day"
joyeux Noël merry Christmas
bonne année happy New Year
joyeuses Pâques happy Easter
meilleurs vœux best wishes
félicitations congratulations
bon appétit have a nice meal, enjoy your meal
bon courage all the best, chin up
bonne chance good luck
à tes (or vos) souhaits bless you (*after a sneeze*)
à la tienne (or la vôtre) cheers
à ta (or votre) santé good health

SURPRISE
---

mon Dieu my goodness
eh bien, eh ben well
comment?, hein?, eh?, quoi? what (was that)?
ah bon oh, I see
ça, par exemple well, well; my word; really
que de . . . what a lot of . . .
sans blague(?) really(?)
ah oui?, c'est vrai?, vraiment? really?
tu rigoles, tu plaisantes you're kidding *or* joking
quelle chance! what a stroke of luck!
tiens! well, well!

POLITENESS
---

s'il vous (*or* te) plaît please; excuse me (*when approaching stranger*)
merci thank you; no, thank you
non merci no thank you; **oui merci** yes please
de rien, je vous en prie, il n'y a pas de quoi not at all, it's quite all right, don't mention it
volontiers willingly, with pleasure

AGREEMENT
---

oui yes
mais oui, bien sûr of course
d'accord O.K., all right
bon, bien fine, O.K.
c'est entendu(?) agreed(?)
soit! [swat] so be it, agreed
justement exactly, that's just it
tant mieux so much the better
ça m'est égal I don't mind, it's all the same to me

DISAGREEMENT

non no; **ah non alors!** oh no!, no no!
mais non no (*contradicting a positive statement*)
si, mais si yes (*contradicting a negative statement*)
bien sûr que non of course not
jamais de la vie never, not on your life
pas du tout not at all, far from it
au contraire on the contrary
tant pis too bad
oh mais non, vraiment really (*exasperated*)
ça, par exemple well I never, well really
quel culot, quel toupet what a cheek, what a nerve
mêlez-vous de vos affaires mind your own business
cela dépend that depends, it all depends
quand même even so; really (*exasperated*), that's a
  bit much
à bas . . . down with . . .

DISTRESS

au secours help; **au feu** fire; **aïe** ouch, ow
hélas alas, oh dear
pardon (I'm) sorry, excuse me, I beg your pardon
je m'excuse I'm sorry (*for having done*)
je regrette I'm sorry
désolé(e) I'm (really) sorry
c'est dommage, quel dommage what a pity
zut, flûte drat, dash it; **mince alors** dash it
j'en ai marre I'm fed up with it
c'en est trop it's (just) too much
je n'en peux plus I can't stand it any more
oh là là oh dear
quelle horreur what a thought; how awful
que faire? what shall I (*or* we) do?
à quoi bon . . . (+ *infinitive*) what's the use of . . .?
que je suis (fatigué etc) how (tired *etc*) I am
c'est embêtant (de . . .) it's embarrassing (to . . .)
ça m'embête it bothers me
ça m'agace it annoys me, it gets on my nerves

ORDERS

attention watch, be careful
halte-là stop
hep *or* **eh, vous là-bas** hey, you there
fiche-moi le camp clear off, clear out
chut shhhh
ça suffit that's enough
défense de (fumer *etc)* no (smoking *etc)*
doucement gently, go easy, easy does it
allons go on, come on
allons-y let's go
allez-y, vas-y on you go, go on, go ahead

OTHERS

ah bon oh well, O.K.
et alors well (*threatening*); so what?, so?
eh bien . . . well . . .
aucune idée no idea
peut-être perhaps, maybe
je ne sais pas I don't know
vous désirez? can I help you?
voici, tiens (*or* **tenez)** here, here you are
voilà there, there you are
j'arrive just coming
ne t'en fais pas don't worry
ce n'est pas la peine it's not worth it
à propos by the way
dis donc (*or* **dites donc)** listen, I say
chéri(e) darling
le (*or* **la) pauvre** poor thing

ESSENTIAL WORDS (m)

le dentiste (m+f)	dentist
le docteur 📖 (m+f)	doctor
l'hôpital (pl hôpitaux)	hospital
un infirmier 📖	(male) nurse
le lit	bed
le malade	patient
le médecin (m+f)	doctor
le rendez-vous (pl inv)	appointment
le sommeil 📖	sleep
le ventre	stomach

IMPORTANT WORDS (m)

l'accident	accident
le brancard	stretcher
le cabinet (de consultation) 📖	surgery
le cachet	tablet
le comprimé	tablet
le coton hydrophile	cotton wool
un coup de soleil	sunburn
le médicament	medicine, drug
le pansement	dressing; bandage
le patient 📖	patient
le pharmacien	chemist
le plâtre ◇	plaster (cast)
le remède 📖	remedy, cure
un rhume	cold
le sang 📖	blood
le sirop	syrup
le sparadrap	sticking plaster

il y a eu un accident there's been an accident
être admis(e) à l'hôpital to be admitted to hospital
vous devez rester au lit you must stay in bed
se sentir malade, être souffrant(e) to feel ill
se sentir mieux to feel better

ESSENTIAL WORDS (f)

une **aspirine**	aspirin
une **infirmière** 📖	nurse
la **pastille**	lozenge
la **pharmacie**	chemist's (shop)
la **santé**	health
la **température**	temperature

IMPORTANT WORDS (f)

une **ambulance**	ambulance
l'**assurance** 📖	insurance
la **blessure**	injury, wound
la **clinique**	clinic, hospital
la **crème** ◇	cream, ointment
la **cuillerée** 📖	spoonful
la **diarrhée**	diarrhoea
la **douleur**	pain
la **fièvre**	fever, (high) temperature
la **grippe**	flu, influenza
une **insolation** 📖	(a touch of) sunstroke
la **maladie**	illness
la **médecine**	(*science of*) medicine
une **opération** 📖	operation
une **ordonnance** ◇	prescription
la **patiente** 📖	patient
la **pilule**	pill; the Pill
la **piqûre**	injection; sting
la **salle de**	
consultation	surgery

je me suis blessé(e), je me suis fait (du) mal I
  have hurt myself
il s'est cassé le bras *etc* he has broken his arm *etc*
je me suis brûlé la main I have burnt my hand
elle s'est coupé le doigt she has cut her finger
**j'ai mal à la gorge/mal aux dents/mal à la tête/
  mal au ventre** I've got a sore throat/toothache/a
  headache/a stomach ache

USEFUL WORDS (m)

un abcès	abscess
un accès	fit
le bandage	bandage
le bleu ◊	bruise
le cancer	cancer
le choc	shock
le dentier	(set of) false teeth
le fauteuil roulant	wheelchair
le fortifiant	tonic
le microbe	germ
le nerf	nerve
un œil (pl yeux) poché	black eye
les oreillons	mumps
le poison	poison
le pouls [pu]	pulse
les premiers secours or	
les premiers soins	first aid
le régime	diet
le repos	rest
le rhume des foins	hayfever
le Sida, SIDA	Aids, AIDS
le sidéen	Aids victim
le vertige	(attack of) dizziness
le virus HIV	HIV virus

j'ai chaud/froid I'm hot/cold
ça me fait mal au cœur it makes me feel sick
maigrir to lose weight; **grossir** to put on weight
avaler to swallow; **saigner** to bleed
se reposer to rest; **guérir** to cure
gravement blessé(e) seriously injured
êtes-vous assuré(e)? are you insured?
remets-toi vite! get well soon!

USEFUL WORDS (f)	
une ampoule ◇	blister
une angine	tonsillitis
une appendicite	appendicitis
la bande ◇	bandage
la béquille	crutch
la cicatrice	scar
la coqueluche	whooping cough
la crise cardiaque	heart attack
une écharde	splinter
une écharpe ◇	sling
une égratignure	scratch
une épidémie	epidemic
la guérison	recovery
une intervention	operation
la maison de retraite	old folks' home
la meurtrissure	bruise
la migraine	migraine
la nausée	sickness, vomiting
l'ouate (hydrophile)	cotton wool
la plaie	wound
la pommade	ointment
la radio(graphie)	X-ray
la rougeole	measles
la rubéole	German measles
la salle ◇ (d'hôpital)	ward
la toux	cough
la transfusion sanguine	blood transfusion
la typhoïde	typhoid
la varicelle	chickenpox
la variole	smallpox

ça me fait mal! that hurts!
faible weak; **fort(e)** strong
respirer to breathe; **hors d'haleine** out of breath
s'évanouir to faint; **tousser** to cough; **mourir** to die
perdre connaissance to lose consciousness

ESSENTIAL WORDS (m)

un ascenseur ⌐	lift
les bagages	luggage
le balcon ◇	balcony
le bar ⌐	bar
le bruit ⌐	noise
le chèque	cheque
le client ◇	resident, guest
le confort ⌐	comfort
le déjeuner	lunch
le directeur ◇	manager
l'escalier	stairs, staircase
un étage	floor; storey
le garçon ◇	waiter
le grand lit	double bed
l'hôtel ◇	hotel
le jour	day
le numéro	number
le passeport	passport
le petit déjeuner	breakfast
le porteur ⌐	porter
le prix ◇	price
le réceptionniste ⌐	receptionist
le repas	meal
le restaurant	restaurant
le rez-de-chaussée	ground floor
le séjour ⌐	stay
le tarif ◇ ⌐	scale of charges, tariff
le téléphone	telephone
le téléviseur (couleur)	(colour) television
les W.-C. ⌐	toilet(s)

je voudrais réserver une chambre I would like to
  book a room
une chambre avec douche/avec salle de bains a
  room with a shower/with a bathroom
une chambre pour une personne a single room
une chambre pour deux personnes a double room

ESSENTIAL WORDS (f)

l'addition	bill
les arrhes 🖙 [aʀ]	deposit
la chambre	room
la clé, clef	key
la cliente ⇨	resident, guest
la date	date
la directrice ⇨	manageress
la douche	shower
l'entrée ⇨	entrance
la fiche 🖙	form, slip
l'hospitalité	hospitality
la (petite) monnaie 🖙	(small) change
la note ⇨	bill
la nuit	night
la pension	guest-house, boarding house
la pension complète	full board
la piscine	swimming pool
la réception 🖙	reception (desk)
la réceptionniste 🖙	receptionist
la réponse	reply
la salle de bains	bathroom
la semaine	week
la serveuse	waitress
la sortie de secours ⇨ 🖙	fire escape
la télévision	television
les toilettes	toilets, "ladies", "gents"
la valise	case, suitcase
la vue 🖙	view

un hôtel de grand luxe a luxury hotel
remplissez cette fiche fill in this form
avez-vous une pièce d'identité? do you have any means of identification?
on a monté les bagages we took the luggage up
on s'est installé we got settled in

IMPORTANT WORDS (m)

l'accueil ⌑	welcome; reception desk
le bouton ◇	switch
le cabinet de toilette	toilet
le chef ◇ (de cuisine) (m+f)	chef, head cook
le guide	guide-book
un incendie ⌑	fire
le Michelin rouge ⌑	(red) Michelin guide
le pourboire ⌑	tip
le prix maximum ⌑	maximum price
le prix minimum ⌑	minimum price
le prix net ⌑	inclusive price
le reçu	receipt

USEFUL WORDS (m)

le cabaret	cabaret
le chasseur ◇	page(-boy)
le cuisinier	cook
un estaminet	"pub"
le foyer	foyer
l'hôtelier	hotelier
le maître d'hôtel	head waiter
le pensionnaire ◇	resident, guest (at boarding house)
le sommelier	wine waiter

occupé(e) occupied; **libre** vacant
propre clean; **sale** dirty
dormir to sleep; **se réveiller** to wake
"tirez" "pull"; **"poussez"** "push"; **"appuyez"** "press"
"tout confort" "with all facilities"

IMPORTANT WORDS (f)

une auberge	inn
la demi-pension	
(pl ~s)	half-board
une étoile 🕮	star
la femme de chambre	chamber maid
la réclamation 🕮	complaint
la salle de télévision	television lounge

USEFUL WORDS (f)

la pension de famille	guest-house, boarding house
la pensionnaire ⇨	resident, guest (at boarding house)
la terrasse	terrace, pavement outside a café

une chambre donnant sur la mer a room overlooking the sea

chambre sans pension room (with no meals)

chambre avec demi-pension room with breakfast and dinner provided

on nous a servis à la terrasse we were served outside

ESSENTIAL WORDS (m)

un appartement	flat
un ascenseur ▢	lift
le balcon ◇	balcony
le bâtiment	building
le chauffage central	central heating
le confort ▢	comfort
le département	*like British county*
un escalier	stairs, staircase
un étage	floor; storey
l'extérieur ▢	exterior, outside
le garage	garage
le grand ensemble ▢	housing estate
un HLM ▢ (habitation à loyer modéré)	council flat *or* house
un immeuble	block of flats
l'intérieur ▢	interior, inside
le jardin	garden
un meuble ▢	a piece of furniture
les meubles ▢	furniture
le mur ▢	wall
le numéro de téléphone	phone number
le parking ◇	parking space
le rez-de-chaussée (pl inv)	ground level, ground floor
le salon	lounge, living room
le sous-sol ▢ (pl ~s)	basement
le terrain ◇ ▢	plot of land
le village	village

j'habite un appartement/une maison jumelle I
live in a flat/a semi-detached
monter/descendre (l'escalier) to go upstairs/
downstairs
en haut upstairs; **en bas** downstairs
les chambres à l'étage the rooms upstairs, the
upstairs rooms

ESSENTIAL WORDS (f)

une adresse	address
une allée	lane
une avenue	avenue
la barrière ⬦	gate; fence
la cave ⌑	cellar
la chambre (à coucher)	bedroom
la clé, clef	key
la cuisine ⬦	kitchen; cooking
la douche	shower
l'entrée ⬦	entrance (hall)
la famille	family
la fenêtre	window
une HLM ⌑ (habitation à loyer modéré)	council flat or house
la maison	house
la pièce ⬦	room
la porte (d'entrée)	(front) door
la rue	street
la salle à manger	dining room
la salle de bains	bathroom
la salle de séjour	living room
la salle ⬦	room
les toilettes	toilet
la ville	town
la vue ⌑	view

à la maison at home, in the house
quand je rentre à la maison when I go home
quand je suis entré(e) dans la salle when I went into the room
regarder par la fenêtre to look out of the window
chez moi/toi/nous/lui *etc* at my/your/our/his *etc* house
déménager to move house; s'installer to settle in
louer une maison to rent a house
faire construire une maison to have a house built

IMPORTANT WORDS (m)

l'aménagement ⌑	fitting out; conversion
l'ameublement ⌑	furniture, furnishing(s)
le cabinet de toilette	toilet
le concierge	caretaker
le couloir ⌑	corridor
le débarras ⌑	box room, junk room
le déménagement	removal
l'entretien ⌑	upkeep; maintenance
le gîte	holiday home
le logement ⌑	lodgings, accommodation
le loyer ⌑	rent
le meuble ⌑	furnished flat or room
le palier ⌑	landing
le propriétaire	owner; landlord
le toit	roof
le voisin	neighbour

USEFUL WORDS (m)

le cabinet de travail	study
le carreau (pl -x)	(floor) tile; (window) pane
le décor ◇	decoration
le grenier ◇	attic
le locataire	tenant; lodger
le parquet	(parquet or wooden) floor
le pavillon ◇	small (detached) house
le plafond	ceiling
le plancher	floor
le seuil	doorstep
le store	blind
le studio	(one-roomed) flatlet
le tuyau (pl -x)	pipe
le vestibule	hall
le volet	shutter

de l'extérieur from the outside
à l'intérieur on the inside
jusqu'au plafond up to the ceiling

IMPORTANT WORDS (f)

la cheminée ⇨ ▢	chimney; fireplace; mantelpiece
la concierge	caretaker
la cour ⇨	yard; courtyard
la femme de ménage	cleaning woman
la fumée	smoke
la pelouse	lawn
la propriétaire	owner; landlady
la voisine	neighbour

USEFUL WORDS (f)

une antenne	aerial
une ardoise	slate
la boue	mud
la chambre d'amis	spare room
la chaudière	boiler
la chaumière	(thatched) cottage
la façade	front (*of house*)
la :haie	hedge
la locataire	tenant; lodger
la loge ⇨	caretaker's room
la lucarne	skylight
la maison jumelle	semi-detached house
la maison secondaire	second *or* holiday home
la mansarde	attic
la marche	step
la ménagère	housewife
la parroi	partition
la porte-fenêtre (*pl* ~s~s)	French window
la sonnette	(door)bell
la tuile	(roof) tile
la vitre	(window) pane

un toit en ardoise a slate roof
frapper à la porte to knock at the door
on a sonné somebody rang (the doorbell)

ESSENTIAL WORDS (m)

le bain ▷	bath
le bouton ▷	switch
le cendrier	ashtray
le dentifrice	toothpaste
le drap ▷ ▭	sheet
un électrophone	record player
un essuie-mains (pl inv)	hand towel
un évier ▭	sink
le feu (pl -x)	fire
le frigidaire, frigo	fridge
le gaz	gas
le lavabo	washbasin
le magnétophone à cassettes	cassette recorder
le magnétoscope	video (recorder)
le ménage	housework
le miroir	mirror
un oreiller ▭	pillow
le placard	cupboard
le plateau ▷ (pl -x)	tray
le poster [pɔstɛʀ]	poster
le radiateur ▭	radiator; heater
le réveil, réveille-matin (pl inv)	alarm clock
les rideaux ▭	curtains
le robinet ▭	tap
le savon	soap
le tableau ▷	the picture
le tapis	carpet, rug
le téléviseur	television set
le transistor	transistor

prendre un bain, se baigner to have a bath
prendre une douche to have a shower
"faire cuire à feu doux" "cook on a low heat"
faire le ménage to do the housework

ESSENTIAL WORDS (f)

une armoire	wardrobe
la balance	weighing scales
la boîte aux lettres ⇨	letterbox
la brosse	brush
la cafetière	coffee pot; coffee maker
la casserole	pan, saucepan
la couverture	rug; blanket; cover
la cuisinière ⇨ ▭	cooker
la douche	shower
l'eau	water
l'électricité	electricity
la glace ⇨	mirror
la lampe	lamp
la lumière ▭	light
la machine à laver ▭	washing machine
la photo	photo
la poubelle	dustbin
la serviette ⇨	towel; napkin, serviette
la télévision	television
la vaisselle	dishes

j'aime faire la cuisine I like (doing the) cooking
faire cuire qch dans une casserole to cook sth in a
   pan
regarder la télévision to watch television
à la télévision on television
allumer/éteindre la télé to switch on/off the TV
jeter qch à la poubelle to throw sth in the dustbin
ouvrir/fermer la lumière to switch on/off the light
faire la vaisselle to do the dishes *or* the washing-up

IMPORTANT WORDS *(m)*	
un aspirateur	vacuum cleaner, Hoover ®
le bidet	bidet
le four	oven
le lave-vaisselle (*pl inv*)	dishwasher
le linge ⟡	bedclothes; washing
le machin	thing, contraption

USEFUL WORDS *(m)*	
le balai	brush, broom
le balai mécanique	carpet sweeper
le bibelot	ornament
le chiffon	duster; rag
le cintre	coat hanger
le coussin	cushion
le couvercle	lid
le fer (à repasser)	iron
le four à micro-ondes	micro-wave oven
le grille-pain (*pl inv*)	toaster
un interrupteur	switch
le mixeur	(electric) mixer
le moulin à café	coffee grinder
le papier peint	wallpaper
le radiateur à accumulation	storage heater
le seau (*pl* -**x**)	bucket
le torchon ⟡	dishcloth
le traversin	bolster
le vase	vase

brancher/débrancher to plug in/to unplug
passer l'aspirateur to hoover round
laver le linge, faire la lessive to do the washing
faire le repassage/le nettoyage to do the ironing/
the cleaning
balayer to sweep (up); **nettoyer** to clean

IMPORTANT WORDS (f)

les affaires ⟡	things
une ampoule ⟡ (électrique)	light bulb
la baignoire	bath
la femme de ménage	cleaning woman
la lessive	washing powder; washing
la peinture ⟡	paint; painting
la poêle [pwal]	frying pan
la poussière	dust
la prise de courant ▢	socket, power point
la recette	recipe
la serrure ▢	lock

USEFUL WORDS (f)

la boîte à ordures	dustbin
la bouilloire	kettle
la cocotte-minute ® (pl ~s~)	pressure cooker
la corbeille ⟡ (à papier)	waste paper basket
la couette	continental quilt, duvet
la couverture chauffante	electric blanket
la descente de lit	bedside rug
la discothèque ⟡	record cabinet or rack
une échelle	ladder
une éponge	sponge
la marmite	pot
la moquette	fitted carpet
les ordures	rubbish, refuse
la planche à repasser	ironing board
la poignée ⟡	handle
la tapisserie ⟡	wallpaper

ranger ses affaires to tidy away one's things
laisser trainer ses affaires to leave one's things
  lying about

ESSENTIAL WORDS (m)

le billet ⟡	ticket; (bank)note
le bureau (pl -x) de change 🞔	bureau de change
le bureau de poste 🞔	post office
le bureau de renseignements	information desk
le centime	centime
le chèque	cheque
le chèque de voyage	traveller's cheque
le code postal	post code
le colis 🞔	parcel, packet
un employé ⟡ 🞔	counter clerk
le facteur 🞔	postman
le franc	franc
le guichet ⟡ 🞔	counter
le nom	name
le numéro	number
le paquet	parcel, packet
le passeport	passport
le prix ⟡	price
les renseignements ⟡	information; directory enquiries
le stylo	pen
le syndicat d'initiative, SI	tourist information office
le tarif 🞔	(postage) rate
le téléphone	telephone
le timbre ⟡, timbre-poste (pl ~s~)	(postage) stamp

je voudrais me renseigner I would like some information

la banque la plus proche the nearest bank

je voudrais encaisser un chèque/changer de l'argent/envoyer une lettre I would like to cash a cheque/change some money/send a letter

---

ESSENTIAL WORDS (f)	

une adresse	address
les arrhes ⌐	deposit
la banque	bank
la boîte aux lettres ▷	postbox, pillarbox
la caisse ▷ ⌐	cash desk; check-out
la carte postale	postcard
une enveloppe	envelope
une erreur	mistake, error
la fiche ⌐	form
la lettre	letter
la livre ▷ **sterling**	pound sterling
la monnaie ⌐	change
les PTT ⌐	*French post and phones*
la pièce d'identité ⌐	(means of) identification
la pièce ▷ ⌐	coin
la poste ▷	post office; post
la réduction ⌐	reduction
la réponse	reply
la signature ⌐	signature

un coup de téléphone *or* **de fil** a phone call
je vais téléphoner à mon père I'm going to phone
  my father
décrocher to lift the receiver
la tonalité the dialling tone
composer le numéro to dial (the number)
l'indicatif (*m*) the (dialling) code
le signal d'appel the ringing tone
allô — ici Jean *or* **c'est Jean à l'appareil** hello —
  this is John
on m'a coupé I've been cut off
la ligne est occupée the line is engaged
ne quittez pas hold the line
patientez, monsieur *or* **mademoiselle** please wait
je me suis trompé(e) de numéro I got the wrong
  number
raccrocher to hang up

IMPORTANT WORDS (m)

un annuaire	telephone directory
le bureau des objets trouvés	lost property office
le carnet de chèques	cheque book
le compte 🕮	account
le coup de téléphone	phone call
le courrier 🕮	mail, letters
le crédit 🕮	credit
le domicile 🕮	home address
le formulaire	form
le jeton 🕮	token (for telephone etc)
le PCV 🕮	reverse-charge call
le paiement 🕮	payment
le papier à lettres	writing paper
le portefeuille	wallet
le porte-monnaie (pl inv)	purse
le supplément	extra charge
le télégramme	telegram

USEFUL WORDS (m)

un aérogramme	airmail letter
l'annuaire des professions	the Yellow Pages
le Bottin	telephone directory
le cadran	dial
le combiné	(telephone) receiver
le destinataire	addressee
l'expéditeur	sender
les fils [fil]	wires
les imprimés	printed matter
le mandat(-poste) (pl ~s~(s))	postal order
le papier d'emballage	wrapping paper
le papier gris	brown paper
le récepteur	(telephone) receiver
le standardiste	(telephone) operator

IMPORTANT WORDS (f)

la cabine téléphonique	callbox
la carte bancaire ▢	bank card
la dépense ▢	expense
la fente ▢	slot
une opératrice ▢	operator
la poste restante	poste restante
la récompense	reward
la taxe ▢	tax

USEFUL WORDS (f)

la bande ◇	wrapper
la carte-lettre (pl ~s~s)	letter-card
la communication interurbaine	trunk call
la communication locale	local call
la dépêche	wire, telegram
la distribution ◇	delivery (of mail)
l'horloge parlante	the speaking clock, TIM
la lettre recommandée	registered letter
la majuscule	block or capital letter
la poste aérienne	airmail
la sonnerie	bell; ringing
la standardiste	switchboard operator
la télécarte	phone card

j'ai perdu mon portefeuille — l'avez-vous trouvé?
  I've lost my wallet — have you found it?
remplir une fiche or **une formule** to fill in a form
en majuscules in block letters
"télécarte: en vente ici" "phonecards on sale here"

GENERAL SITUATIONS

quelle est votre adresse? what is your address?
comment cela s'écrit? how do you write (*or* spell) that?
avez-vous la monnaie de . . .? do you have change of . . .?
écrire to write; **répondre** to reply; **signer** to sign
est-ce que vous pouvez m'aider? can you help me please?
pour aller à la gare . . .? how do I get to the station?
tout droit straight on
à droite to *or* on the right; **à gauche** to *or* on the left
derrière behind; **devant** in front (+ of *when prep*)
en face (+ de *when prep*) opposite; **vers** towards

le nord: au nord	north: in *or* to the north
le sud: au sud	south: in *or* to the south
l' est (*m*): **à l'est**	east: in *or* to the east
l' ouest (*m*): **à l'ouest**	west: in *or* to the west

LETTERS

Cher Robert Dear Robert; **Chère Anne** Dear Anne
Cher Monsieur Dear Sir; **Chère Madame** (*or* **Mademoiselle**) Dear Madam
amitiés very best wishes or regards
bien affectueusement (à vous) yours affectionately
bien amicalement *or* **cordialement (à vous)** yours ever
bons baisers love and kisses; **ton ami(e)** your friend
veuillez agréer mes (*or* **nos**) **salutations distinguées** yours faithfully
je vous prie d'agréer, Monsieur (*or* **Madame** *etc*) **l'expression de mes sentiments les meilleurs** yours sincerely
T.S.V.P. P.T.O.

PRONUNCIATION GUIDE

When you are talking on the phone or giving details to
someone you are often asked to spell something out.
This is how you go about it in French. For further
information on the International Phonetic Alphabet
(IPA) symbols used in column 2, see page 7.

	Phonetically	*Pronounced approximately as*
A	[a]	**ah**
B	[be]	**bay**
C	[se]	**say**
D	[de]	**day**
E	[ə]	**ay**
F	[ɛf]	**ef**
G	[ʒe]	**zhay**
H	[aʃ]	**ash**
I	[i]	**ee**
J	[ʒi]	**zhee**
K	[ka]	**kah**
L	[ɛl]	**el**
M	[ɛm]	**em**
N	[ɛn]	**en**
O	[o]	**oh**
P	[pe]	**pay**
Q	[ky]	**koo**
R	[ɛr]	**air**
S	[ɛs]	**ess**
T	[te]	**tay**
U	[y]	**oo**
V	[ve]	**vay**
W	[dublə ve]	**dooble-vay**
X	[iks]	**eeks**
Y	[i grek]	**ee grek**
Z	[zɛd]	**zed**

Try it out with your own name and the names of
some friends.

ESSENTIAL WORDS (m)

un **agent (de police)**	policeman
l'**argent** ◇	silver; money
le **bulletin d'informations**	news bulletin
le **chèque (de voyage)**	(traveller's) cheque
le **commissariat de police**	police station
un **incendie**	fire
l'**or**	gold
le **problème**	problem
le **type**	fellow, chap

IMPORTANT WORDS (m)

un **accident**	accident
le **budget** ▭	budget
le **bureau des objets trouvés**	lost property office
le **cambrioleur**	burglar, robber
le **constat**	report
le **consulat**	consulate
le(s) **dommage(s)**	damage
un **espion**	spy
le **gendarme**	gendarme
le **gouvernement**	government
le **manifestant**	demonstrator
le **mort** ◇	dead man
le **porte-monnaie** (*pl inv*)	purse
le **portefeuille**	wallet
le **poste de police**	police station
le **propriétaire**	owner
le **témoin** ▭	witness
le **vol** ◇	robbery
le **voleur**	robber, thief

---

voler to steal; to rob; **cambrioler** to burgle
j'ai été volé! I've been robbed!

ESSENTIAL WORDS (f)

la banque	bank
la faute ◇ ⊞	fault
une identité	identity
la pièce d'identité ⊞	(means of) identification

IMPORTANT WORDS (f)

une amende ⊞	fine
une armée	army
la bande ◇	gang
la gendarmerie	headquarters of gendarmes
la manifestation ⊞	demonstration
la mort ◇	death
la morte	dead woman
la peine de mort	death penalty
la permission	permission
la police d'assurance	insurance policy
la police-secours	emergency services
la propriétaire	owner
la récompense	reward
la taxe ⊞	tax

contre la loi against the law; illegal
ce n'est pas de ma faute it's not my fault
au secours! help!; **à l'assassin!** murder!
au voleur! stop thief!; **au feu!** fire!
haut les mains! hands up!
dévaliser une banque to rob a bank
manifester to demonstrate, stage a demonstration
récompenser to reward

USEFUL WORDS (m)

un **agent secret**	secret agent
un **assassin**	murderer
le **butin**	loot
le **cadavre**	corpse
le **coup (de fusil)**	(gun) shot
le **courage**	bravery
le **crime**	crime
le **criminel**	criminal
le **détective privé**	private detective
le **détournement**	hijacking
le **drogué**	drug addict
un **enlèvement**	kidnapping
un **escroc** [ɛskʀo]	crook
le **flic**	"cop"
le **fusil** [fyzi]	gun
le **gangster**	gangster
le **garde**	guard
le **gardien** ⇨	guard; warden, attendant
le **:héros**	hero
un **hold-up** (*pl inv*)	hold-up
le **juge**	judge
le **jury**	jury
le **meurtre**	murder
le **meurtrier**	murderer
un **otage**	hostage
le **palais de justice**	law courts
le **pirate de l'air**	hijacker
le **policier**	policeman
le **prisonnier**	prisoner
le **procès**	trial
le **reportage**	report
le **révolutionnaire**	revolutionary
le **revolver** [ʀevɔlvɛʀ]	revolver
le **sauvetage**	rescue
le **terrorisme**	terrorism
le **terroriste**	terrorist
le **voyou**	hooligan

USEFUL WORDS (f)

l'accusation	the prosecution
une accusation	charge; accusation
une agglomération	built-up area
une arme	weapon
une arrestation	arrest
la bagarre	fight, scuffle
la bombe	bomb
la cellule	cell
la défense ⇨	defence
la déposition	statement
la dispute	argument, dispute
la droguée	drug addict
les drogues	drugs
une émeute	uprising
une enquête	inquiry
une évasion	escape
l'héroïne	heroine
l'incarcération	imprisonment
la loi	law
une ordonnance ⇨	decree, police order
la pancarte	placard
la preuve	proof
la prise (de)	capture (of)
la prison	prison
la rafle	raid
la rançon	ransom
la révolution	revolution
la tentative	attempt

une attaque à main armée an armed robbery *or* hold-up
détourner un avion to hijack a plane
enlever un enfant to kidnap *or* abduct a child
se battre to fight; **se disputer** to quarrel
une bande de voyous a bunch of hooligans
en prison in prison

ESSENTIAL WORDS (m)

l'argent ◇	silver
le bois ⌂	wood
le coton ⌂	cotton
le cuir	leather
le gas-oil ⌂	diesel
le gaz	gas
le jean [dʒin]	denim
le métal ⌂	
(*pl* métaux)	metal
le nylon ⌂	nylon
l'or	gold
le plastique ⌂	plastic
le verre	glass

IMPORTANT WORDS (m)

l'aluminium	aluminium
le coton hydrophile	cotton wool
l'état	condition
le papier	paper
le pétrole	oil, petroleum; paraffin

une chaise *etc* **de** *or* **en bois** a wooden chair *etc*
une boîte en plastique a plastic box
une bague d'or *or* **en or/d'argent** a gold/silver ring
en bon état in good condition; **en mauvais état** in
  bad condition
les bottes (*fpl*) **de caoutchouc** wellington boots
le papier d'étain tinfoil, silver paper
le papier hygiénique toilet paper
le fer forgé wrought iron

ESSENTIAL WORDS (f)

la corde ▷	rope
l'essence 🕮	petrol
la fourrure	fur
l'huile	oil
la laine 🕮	wool
la pierre	stone

IMPORTANT WORDS (f)

la brique	brick
la soie	silk

un manteau en fourrure a fur coat
un pull en laine a woolly jumper

USEFUL (m)

l'acier	steel
l'acrylique	acrylic (fibre)
le béton	concrete
le bronze	bronze
le caoutchouc [kautʃu]	rubber
le caoutchouc mousse	foam rubber
le carton	cardboard
le charbon	coal
le ciment	cement
le cristal	crystal
le cuivre	copper
le cuivre jaune	brass
le daim	suede
le drap ◇	woollen cloth
l'étain	tin; pewter
le fer	iron
le fer-blanc (pl ~s~s)	tin, tinplate
le fil	thread
le fil de fer	wire
le granit	granite
le lin	flax
le liquide	liquid
le marbre	marble
les matériaux	materials
l'osier	wickerwork
le plâtre ◇	plaster
le plomb	lead
le satin	satin
le suède	suede
le tergal ®	terylene ®
le tissu	cloth, material
le tweed	tweed
le velours	velvet
le velours côtelé	cord, corduroy
le vinyle	vinyl

USEFUL WORDS (f)

l'argile	clay
la cire	wax
la colle ◊	glue
la dentelle	lace
l'étoffe	material
la faïence	earthenware, pottery
la ficelle	string
la :houille	(industrial) coal
la paille ◊	straw
la peau de mouton	sheepskin
la peau de porc	pigskin
la porcelaine	porcelain, china
la toile	linen; canvas

un bout de ficelle a piece of string
un chapeau de paille a straw hat

ESSENTIAL WORDS (m)

le groupe	group
un orchestre ◇	orchestra

IMPORTANT WORDS (m)

le chef d'orchestre	conductor
un instrument de	
musique ☐	musical instrument
le musicien ☐	musician
le piano	piano
le saxophone	saxophone
le trombone	trombone
le violon	violin, fiddle

USEFUL WORDS (m)

un accord ◇	chord
un accordéon	accordion
le basson	bassoon
le bâton ◇	conductor's baton
le clairon	bugle
le cor d'harmonie	French horn
l'harmonica	harmonica, mouth organ
le :hautbois	oboe
le jazz [dʒaz]	jazz
un orgue	organ
le soliste	soloist
le tambour	drum
le tambourin	tambourine
le triangle	triangle
le violoncelle	cello
le xylophone [ksilɔfɔn]	xylophone

écoutez la musique! listen to the music!
**jouer du piano/de la guitare/du violon/de la
   batterie** to play the piano/the guitar/the violin/the
   drums
travailler son piano to practise the piano

ESSENTIAL WORDS (f)	
la musique	music

IMPORTANT WORDS (f)	
la clarinette	clarinet
la flûte	flute
la flûte à bec	recorder
la guitare	guitar

USEFUL WORDS (f)	
la batterie ⬦	drums, drum kit
la contrebasse	double bass
la corde ⬦	string
la cornemuse	bagpipes
les cymbales	cymbals
la fanfare	brass band; fanfare
la grosse caisse	big drum, bass drum
la :harpe	harpe
la note ⬦	note
la salle des fêtes	concert hall
la soliste	soloist
la touche ⬦	(piano) key
la trompette	trumpet

jouer or **interpréter un morceau** to play a piece
jouer fort to play loudly; **jouer doucement** to play softly
une fausse note a wrong note
jouer/chanter juste to play/sing in tune
jouer/chanter faux to play/sing off key

CARDINAL NUMBERS		
nought	0	zéro
one	1	(m) un, (f) une
two	2	deux
three	3	trois
four	4	quatre
five	5	cinq
six	6	six
seven	7	sept
eight	8	huit
nine	9	neuf
ten	10	dix
eleven	11	onze
twelve	12	douze
thirteen	13	treize
fourteen	14	quatorze
fifteen	15	quinze
sixteen	16	seize
seventeen	17	dix-sept
eighteen	18	dix-huit
nineteen	19	dix-neuf
twenty	20	vingt
twenty-one	21	vingt et un
twenty-two	22	vingt-deux
twenty-three	23	vingt-trois
thirty	30	trente
thirty-one	31	trente et un
thirty-two	32	trente-deux
forty	40	quarante
fifty	50	cinquante
sixty	60	soixante
seventy	70	soixante-dix
seventy-one	71	soixante-et-onze
eighty	80	quatre-vingts
eighty-one	81	quatre-vingt-un
ninety	90	quatre-vingt-dix
ninety-one	91	quatre-vingt-onze
a (or one) hundred	100	cent

CARDINAL NUMBERS (cont)		
a hundred and one	**101**	cent un
a hundred and two	**102**	cent deux
a hundred and ten	**110**	cent dix
a hundred and eighty-two	**182**	cent-quatre-vingt-deux
two hundred	**200**	deux cents
two hundred and one	**201**	deux cent un
two hundred and two	**202**	deux cent deux
three hundred	**300**	trois cents
four hundred	**400**	quatre cents
five hundred	**500**	cinq cents
six hundred	**600**	six cents
seven hundred	**700**	sept cents
eight hundred	**800**	huit cents
nine hundred	**900**	neuf cents
a (*or* one) thousand	**1000**	mille
a thousand and one	**1001**	mille un
a thousand and two	**1002**	mille deux
two thousand	**2000**	deux mille
ten thousand	**10000**	dix mille
a (*or* one) hundred thousand	**100000**	cent mille
a (*or* one) million	**1000000**	un million
two million	**2000000**	deux millions

N.B. 1000000: In French, the word *million* is a noun, so the numeral takes *de* when there is a following noun: *un million de gens, trois millions de maisons*

ORDINAL NUMBERS

first	1	(*m*) premier, (*f*) -ière
second	2	deuxième
third	3	troisième
fourth	4	quatrième
fifth	5	cinquième
sixth	6	sixième
seventh	7	septième
eighth	8	huitième
ninth	9	neuvième
tenth	10	dixième
eleventh	11	onzième
twelfth	12	douzième
thirteenth	13	treizième
fourteenth	14	quatorzième
fifteenth	15	quinzième
sixteenth	16	seizième
seventeenth	17	dix-septième
eighteenth	18	dix-huitième
nineteenth	19	dix-neuvième
twentieth	20	vingtième
twenty-first	21	vingt et unième
twenty-second	22	vingt-deuxième
thirtieth	30	trentième
thirty-first	31	trente et unième
fortieth	40	quarantième
fiftieth	50	cinquantième
sixtieth	60	soixantième
seventieth	70	soixante-dixième
eightieth	80	quatre-vingtième
ninetieth	90	quatre-vingt-dixième
hundredth	100	centième

ORDINAL NUMBERS (cont)

hundred and first	**101**	cent unième
hundred and tenth	**110**	cent-dixième
two hundredth	**200**	deux centième
three hundredth	**300**	trois centième
four hundredth	**400**	quatre centième
five hundredth	**500**	cinq centième
six hundredth	**600**	six centième
seven hundredth	**700**	sept centième
eight hundredth	**800**	huit centième
nine hundredth	**900**	neuf centième
thousandth	**1000**	millième
two thousandth	**2000**	deux millième
millionth	**1000000**	millionième
two millionth	**2000000**	deux millionième

FRACTIONS

a half	$\frac{1}{2}$	(m) un demi,
		(f) une demie
one and a half helpings	$1\frac{1}{2}$	une portion et demie
two and a half kilos	$2\frac{1}{2}$	deux kilos et demi
a third	$\frac{1}{3}$	un tiers
two thirds	$\frac{2}{3}$	deux tiers
a quarter	$\frac{1}{4}$	un quart
three quarters	$\frac{3}{4}$	trois quarts
a sixth	$\frac{1}{6}$	un sixième
five and five sixths	$5\frac{5}{6}$	cinq et cinq sixièmes
a twelfth	$\frac{1}{12}$	un douzième
seven twelfths	$\frac{7}{12}$	sept douzièmes
a hundredth	$\frac{1}{100}$	un centième
a thousandth	$\frac{1}{1000}$	un millième

une assiette de a plate of
une bande de a group *or* gang of; a flock of (*birds*)
beaucoup de (monde) lots of (people)
une boîte de a tin *or* can of; a box of
un bol de a bowl of
une bouchée de a mouthful of
un bout de papier a bit *or* piece of paper
une bouteille de a bottle of
cent grammes (*mpl*) de a hundred grammes of
une centaine de (about) a hundred
une cuillerée de a spoonful of
un demi de bière half a litre of beer, "a half"
une demi-douzaine de half a dozen
un demi-kilo de half a kilo of
un demi-litre de half a litre of
tous (*f* toutes) les deux both of them
une dizaine de (about) ten
une douzaine de a dozen
une foule de a crowd of, crowds of, heaps of, masses
of
un kilo(gramme) de a kilo(gramme) of
à quelques kilomètres de a few kilometres from
un litre de a litre of
une livre ⬦ de a pound of
un mètre de a metre of
à quelques mètres de a few metres from
des milliers de thousands of
la moitié de half of
un morceau de sucre a lump of sugar
un morceau de gâteau a piece *or* slice of cake
une paire de a pair of
un paquet de a packet of
une partie ⬦ de a part of
un peu de a little, a trifle
une pile de a pile of
la plupart de *or* **des** most (of)
plusieurs (des) several (of)
une poignée ⬦ de a handful of

une portion de a portion *or* helping of
un pot de a pot *or* tub; a jar of
(une) quantité de a lot of, many; a quantity of
un quart de a quarter of
une tablette de a bar of (*chocolate*)
un tas de a heap of, heaps of
une tasse de a cup(ful) of
un tonneau de a barrel of
une tranche de a slice of
trois quarts de three quarters of
un troupeau de a herd of (*cattle*); a flock of (*sheep*)
un verre de a glass of

ESSENTIAL WORDS (m)

l'argent ◇	silver; money
le miroir	mirror
l'or	gold
le parfum ◇ ▢	perfume, scent
le rasoir ▢	razor

IMPORTANT WORDS (m)

le bijou (*pl* **-x**)	jewel
le bracelet	bracelet, bangle
le déodorant	deodorant
le gant de toilette	face flannel
le maquillage ▢	make-up
le peigne	comb
le salon de beauté	beauty salon *or* parlour
le shampooing [ʃɑ̃pwɛ̃]	shampoo

USEFUL WORDS (m)

le bigoudi	curler, roller
le blaireau (*pl* **-x**)	shaving brush
le bouton de manchette	cufflink
le collier	necklace, beads
le diamant	diamond
le dissolvant	nail varnish remover
les effets personnels	personal effects
le fard	make-up
le fard à paupières	eye-shadow
le fond de teint	foundation
le kleenex ®	(paper) tissue
le pendentif	pendant
le porte-clefs (*pl inv*)	key-ring
le poudrier	(powder) compact
le rimmel	mascara
le rouge à lèvres	lipstick
le vernis à ongles	nail varnish, nail polish

ESSENTIAL WORDS (f)	
la brosse à dents	toothbrush
la pâte dentifrice	toothpaste

IMPORTANT WORDS (f)	
la bague	ring
la beauté	beauty
la chaîne	chain
la chaînette	chain
la crème de beauté	face cream
l'eau de toilette	toilet water
la glace ◇	mirror
la montre	watch

USEFUL WORDS (f)	
une **alliance**	wedding ring
la boucle d'oreille	
(pl ~s d'oreille)	earring
la broche	brooch
la coiffure	hairstyle
la crème à raser	shaving cream
une **éponge**	sponge
la gourmette	identity bracelet
la manucure	manicure
la perle	pearl
la perruque	wig
la poudre (de riz)	face powder

se laver to get washed; **s'habiller** to get dressed
se farder, se maquiller to put on one's make-up
se démaquiller to take off one's make-up
se coiffer to do one's hair
se brosser les cheveux to brush one's hair
se peigner to comb one's hair
se raser to shave; **se brosser les dents** to brush
  one's teeth
prêt(e) à partir ready to leave

ESSENTIAL WORDS (m)

un arbre	tree
le jardin	garden
le jardinage	gardening
le jardinier	gardener
les légumes	vegetables
le parfum ⇨ 🕮	perfume, scent
le soleil ⇨	sun

IMPORTANT WORDS (m)

le banc (de jardin)	(garden) seat
le bouquet de fleurs	bunch of flowers

un jardin entouré d'arbres a garden surrounded by trees

offrir un bouquet de fleurs à qn to give sb a bunch of flowers

tondre le gazon to mow the lawn

"défense de marcher sur le gazon" "keep off the grass"

mon père aime jardiner my father likes gardening

planter to plant; **déplanter** to dig up

ESSENTIAL WORDS (f)

une abeille	bee
la branche	branch
la feuille	leaf
la fleur	flower
l'herbe 📖	grass
la pelouse	lawn
la pierre	stone, rock
la pluie	rain
la rose ⇨	rose
la terre	earth, ground

IMPORTANT WORDS (f)

la barrière ⇨	gate; fence
la culture ⇨	cultivation
la guêpe	wasp
la plante	plant

les fleurs poussent the flowers grow
par terre on the ground
cueillir des fleurs to pick flowers
se mettre à l'ombre to go into the shade
rester à l'ombre to remain in the shade
à l'ombre d'un arbre in the shade of a tree
la guêpe va vous piquer the wasp is going to sting
  you

USEFUL WORDS (m)

un **arbuste**	shrub, bush
un **arrosoir**	watering can
le **bassin**	(ornamental) pool
le **bourgeon**	bud
le **bouton-d'or** (pl ~**s**~)	buttercup
le **buisson**	bush
le **chèvrefeuille**	honeysuckle
le **chrysanthème**	chrysanthemum
le **coquelicot**	poppy
le **crocus**	crocus
le **feuillage**	leaves
le **gazon**	lawn; turf
l'**hortensia**	hydrangea
le **jardin potager**	vegetable garden
le **lierre**	ivy
le **lilas**	lilac
le **lis** [lis]	lily
le **muguet**	lily of the valley
un **œillet**	carnation
un **outil**	tool
le **papillon**	butterfly
le **parterre** ⟡	border, flower bed
le **pavillon** ⟡	summer house
le **pavot**	poppy
le **perce-neige** (pl inv)	snowdrop
le **pissenlit**	dandelion
le **pois de senteur**	sweet pea
le **rosier**	rose bush
le **sol**	earth, soil
le **soleil** ⟡, **tournesol**	sunflower
le **tronc**	trunk (of tree)
le **tuyau d'arrosage**	hose
le **ver**	worm
le **verger**	orchard

USEFUL WORDS (f)	
une **allée**	path
la **baie** ⇨	berry
la **brouette**	wheelbarrow
la **clôture**	fence
une **échelle**	ladder
une **épine**	thorn
la **giroflée jaune**	wallflower
les **graines**	seeds
la **:haie**	hedge
la **jacinthe**	hyacinth
la **jonquille**	daffodil
la **marguerite**	daisy
les **mauvaises herbes**	weeds
une **ombre**	shadow
une **orchidée**	orchid
la **pâquerette**	daisy
la **pensée** ⇨	pansy
la **pivoine**	peony
la **plate-bande** (pl ~s~s)	flower bed
la **primevère**	primrose
la **racine**	root
la **renoncule**	buttercup
la **rocaille**	rockery, rock garden
la **rosée**	dew
la **semence**	seed (in general)
la **serre**	greenhouse
la **tige**	stalk
la **tondeuse**	lawnmower
la **tulipe**	tulip
la **violette**	violet

ESSENTIAL WORDS (m)

le baigneur	bather, swimmer
le bain ⟡ (de mer)	bathe (in sea), swim
le bateau (pl -x) de pêche	fishing boat
le bikini	bikini
le bord de la mer	seaside
le maillot ⟡ (de bain)	swimming costume or trunks
le passager	passenger
le pêcheur	fisherman
le pique-nique (pl ~s) 🕮	picnic
le pont ⟡	deck (of ship)
le port	port, harbour
le prix du billet	fare
le quai ⟡ [ke]	quay, quayside
le slip de bain	swimming or bathing trunks

IMPORTANT WORDS (m)

le château (pl -x) de sable	sandcastle
le coup de soleil	sunstroke
le crabe	crab
le fond	bottom
l'horizon	horizon
le mal de mer	seasickness
le matelas pneumatique	airbed, lilo
le sable	sand
le téléscope	telescope
le vacancier	holiday-maker

au bord de la mer at the seaside
faire un pique-nique to go for a picnic
à l'horizon on the horizon
il a le mal de mer he is (feeling) sea-sick

ESSENTIAL WORDS (f)

une agence de voyages	travel agent's
la brochure	brochure
la côte ◇	coast
l'eau	water
une île	island
les lunettes de soleil	sunglasses
la mer	sea
la natation ▭	swimming
la passagère	passenger
la pierre	stone, rock
la plage	beach
la promenade ◇	trip, outing; walk
la serviette ◇	towel

IMPORTANT WORDS (f)

la chaise longue	deckchair
la crème solaire	sun(-tan) cream
la traversée	crossing

nager to swim; **se noyer** to drown
regarder les brochures to look at brochures
nous allons à la côte aujourd'hui we're going to the coast today
je vais me baigner I'm going for a swim
plonger dans l'eau to dive into the water; **flotter** to float
au fond de la mer at the bottom of the sea
à la plage on the beach; to the beach
faire la traversée en bateau to cross over by boat
se bronzer to get a tan

USEFUL WORDS (m)

l'air marin	sea air
un aviron	oar
le bac ⇨	ferry(-boat)
le caillou (pl -x)	pebble
le cap [kap]	point
le coquillage	shell
le courant	current
un équipage	crew
les flots	waves
le gouvernail	rudder
le maître nageur	lifeguard
le marin	sailor
le mât	mast
le matelot	sailor
le naufrage	shipwreck
les naufragés	people who are shipwrecked
un océan	ocean
le pavillon ⇨	flag
le pédalo	pedal-boat
le phare ⇨	lighthouse
le port de plaisance	marina
le radeau (pl -x)	raft
le rivage	coast, shore
le rocher	rock
le seau (pl -x)	bucket
le vaisseau (pl -x)	vessel
le vapeur ⇨	steamer

USEFUL WORDS (f)

les algues	seaweed
une ancre	anchor
la baie ⋄	bay
la barque	small boat
la bouée	buoy
la cargaison	cargo
la ceinture de sauvetage	lifebelt
la cheminée ⋄	funnel
la croisière	cruise
l'écume	foam
une embouchure	mouth (*of river*)
une épave	wreck
la falaise	cliff
la flotte	fleet
une insolation	(touch of) sunstroke
la jetée	pier, jetty
les jumelles ⋄	binoculars
la marée	tide
la marine	navy
la mouette	seagull
la passerelle	gangway; bridge (*of ship*)
la pelle ⋄	spade
la rame	oar
la vague	wave
la voile ⋄	sail; sailing

se promener au bord des falaises to walk at the edge of the cliffs
j'ai eu une insolation I had a touch of sunstroke
à marée basse/haute at low/high tide
faire de la voile to go sailing

ESSENTIAL WORDS (m)	
l'argent ◇	money
un ascenseur 🕮	lift
le boucher 🕮	butcher
le boulanger 🕮	baker
le bureau (pl -x) de poste 🕮	post office
le bureau de tabac	tobacconist's (shop)
le cadeau (pl -x)	present
le café ◇	café
le café-tabac	café (which sells tobacco)
le centime	centime
le centre commercial 🕮	shopping centre
le charcutier 🕮	pork butcher
le chèque	cheque
le client ◇	customer, client
un employé ◇ 🕮	employee; clerk
un épicier 🕮	grocer
un étage	floor
le franc	franc
le grand magasin	department store
l'hypermarché 🕮	hypermarket
le magasin	shop
le magasin de chaussures	shoe shop
le marché ◇	market; deal
le pâtissier	confectioner, pastrycook
le prix ◇	price
le rayon ◇ 🕮	department, counter
le rez-de-chaussée (pl inv)	ground level, ground floor
les soldes 🕮	sales; bargains
le sous-sol 🕮 (pl ~s)	basement
le souvenir	souvenir
le supermarché	supermarket
le tabac ◇	tobacconist's
le vendeur 🕮	shop assistant, salesman

ESSENTIAL WORDS (f)	
l'addition	bill
une agence de voyages	travel agent's
une alimentation 🗀	food store
la banque	bank
la boucherie	butcher's (shop)
la boulangerie	baker's (shop)
la boutique 🗀	small shop
la caisse ◇	till; cash desk; check-out
la charcuterie 🗀	pork butcher's
la cliente ◇	customer, client
la crémerie 🗀	dairy
une employée ◇ 🗀	employee
une épicerie	grocer's (shop)
une erreur	mistake, error
la liste	list
la (petite) monnaie 🗀	(small) change
la parfumerie 🗀	perfume shop/counter/department
la pâtisserie ◇	cake shop, confectioner's
la pharmacie	chemist's (shop)
la pointure 🗀	(shoe) size
la poste ◇	post office
la réduction	reduction
la saison des soldes	sales-time
la taille ◇	size
la vendeuse 🗀	shop assistant, salesgirl

acheter/vendre qch to buy/sell sth
il a envie d'acheter une voiture/de vendre sa voiture he would like to buy a car/to sell his car
quel est le prix de ce manteau? what is the price of this coat?
ça coûte combien? how much does this cost?
ça fait combien? how much does that come to?
je l'ai payé(e) 5 francs I paid 5 francs for it
chez le boucher/le boulanger at the butcher's/baker's

IMPORTANT WORDS (m)

un **article**	article
le **cabinet de consultation**	surgery
le **coiffeur**	hairdresser; barber
le **commerçant** 🗍	tradesman
le **commerce**	trade, business
le **comptoir** 🗍	counter
le **cordonnier** 🗍	cobbler
un **escalier roulant** 🗍	escalator
le **gérant** 🗍	manager
le **libre-service** 🗍 (*pl* ~s~s)	self-service store *or* restaurant
le **marchand de fruits** 🗍	fruiterer
le **marchand de légumes** 🗍	greengrocer
le **portefeuille**	wallet
le **porte-monnaie** (*pl inv*)	purse
le **reçu**	receipt

il doit y avoir une erreur there must be some mistake
je ne fais que regarder I'm just looking
c'est trop cher it's too expensive
quelque chose de moins cher something cheaper
c'est bon marché it's (very) cheap
c'est mieux marché it's cheaper
"payez à la caisse" "pay at the cash desk"
j'ai trop dépensé I've spent too much money
c'est pour offrir? is it for a present? (*i.e.* would you like it gift-wrapped?)
avec ça? anything else?

IMPORTANT WORDS (f)	
la **bibliothèque** ⇨	library
la **cordonnerie**	cobbler's
la **laverie**	
automatique	launderette
la **librairie**	bookshop
la **promotion** 📖	special offer
la **réclamation** 📖	complaint
la **vitrine**	shop window

S.A. (société anonyme) Ltd.
S.A.R.L. (société à responsabilité limitée) limited
  liability company
et Cie & Co.
"en vente ici" "on sale here"
"maison à vendre" "house for sale"
"appartement à louer" "flat to rent"
"souris à donner" "mice free to good home"
une voiture d'occasion a second-hand car

USEFUL WORDS (*m*)

un **agent de tourisme**	travel agent
un **agent immobilier**	estate agent
le **bibliothécaire**	librarian
le **bijoutier**	jeweller
le **bon**	form, coupon
le **bookmaker**	bookmaker
le **coloris**	colour
le **confiseur**	confectioner
le **débit de fritures**	fish-and-chip shop
le **débit de tabac**	tobacconist's
le **disquaire**	record-dealer
l'**horloger**	watchmaker
le **libraire**	bookseller
le **mannequin** ⟡	dummy, model
le **marchand de biens**	estate agent
le **marchand de journaux**	newsagent
le **marchand de nouveautés**	draper
le **marchand de poissons**	fishmonger
le **marchand des quatre saisons**	barrow-boy, costermonger
un **opticien**	optician
le **produit**	product; (*pl*) produce
le **pub**	pub
le **quincaillier**	ironmonger
le **tailleur** ⟡	tailor
le **vidéoclub**	video shop
le **zinc**	counter (*of bar or pub*)

USEFUL WORDS (f)

une **agence immobilière**	estate agent's
la **bijouterie**	jeweller's (shop)
la **blanchisserie**	laundry, dry cleaner's
la **boutique d'animaux**	pet shop
la **caisse d'épargne**	savings bank
les **commissions**	shopping
la **compagnie**	company
la **compagnie d'assurance**	insurance company
la **confiserie**	sweetshop, confectioner's
une **course** ◇	errand
les **courses**	shopping
la **devanture**	shop window; display
la **droguerie**	dispensing chemist's
une **encolure**	collar size
l'**horlogerie**	watchmaker's
la **laiterie**	dairy
la **maison de commerce**	firm
la **maison de couture**	fashion house
les **marchandises**	goods, wares
la **papeterie**	stationer's
la **queue** ◇ [kø]	queue
la **quincaillerie**	ironmonger's, hardware shop
la **société d'assurance**	insurance company
la **société de crédit immobilier**	building society
la **succursale**	branch
la **teinturerie**	dry-cleaner's
la **vente**	sale; selling; sales

faire les courses to go shopping

ESSENTIAL WORDS (m)

le badminton	badminton
le ballon ⇨	(foot)ball
le basket(ball)	basketball
le billard	billiards
le but [byt]	goal
le champion	champion
le championnat	championship
le cricket	cricket
le cyclisme 🕮	cycling
le football	football (*game*)
le golf	golf
le :hockey	hockey
le jeu ⇨ (*pl* -x)	game; play
le joueur	player
le match (*pl* matches)	game; match
le netball	netball
le résultat	result
le rugby	rugby
le ski	skiing; ski
le sport	sport
le stade	stadium
le Tour de France	Tour de France (*cycle race*)
le tennis	tennis; tennis court
le terrain ⇨ (de sport)	ground; pitch; course
le volley-ball (*pl* ~s)	volleyball

jouer au football/au tennis *etc* to play football/ tennis *etc*
marquer un but/un point to score a goal/a point
marquer les points to keep the score
le champion du monde the world champion
gagner/perdre un match to win/lose a match
j'ai gagné/perdu! I won/lost!
faire match nul to draw (*in a match*)
mon sport préféré my favourite sport

ESSENTIAL WORDS (f)	
la **championne**	champion
une **équipe**	team
l'**équitation**	horse-riding
la **gymnastique**	gymnastics
la **joueuse**	player
la **natation** 📖	swimming
la **partie** ◇	game
la **pêche** ◇	fishing
la **piscine**	swimming pool
la **planche à voile**	windsurfing; windsurfer (board)
la **promenade** ◇	walk
la **voile** ◇	sailing

courir to run; **sauter** to jump; **lancer, jeter** to throw
battre qn to beat sb; **s'entraîner** to train
mener to be in the lead
je suis un supporter du Liverpool I support Liverpool
une partie de tennis a game of tennis
il fait partie d'un club he belongs to a club
aller à la pêche to go fishing
aller à la piscine to go to the swimming pool
sais-tu nager? can you swim?
faire une promenade en vélo to go for a ride on one's bike
faire de la voile to go sailing
faire du footing/de l'alpinisme to go jogging/ climbing

IMPORTANT WORDS (m)

le gardien de but	goalkeeper
le maillot ◇	(football) jersey

USEFUL WORDS (m)

un adversaire	opponent
l'alpinisme	mountaineering
un arbitre	referee; (*tennis*) umpire
l'athlétisme	athletics
le canotage	rowing
le catch	wrestling
le champ de course	race course
le chronomètre	stopwatch
le chronométreur	timekeeper
le débutant	beginner
le détenteur (du titre)	(title-)holder
un entraîneur	trainer, coach
le filet ◇	net
le footing	jogging
le gymnase	gymnasium, gym
l'hippisme	horse-racing; horse-riding
les Jeux olympiques	the Olympic Games
le javelot	javelin
le patin (à roulettes)	(roller) skate
le rallye (automobile)	(car) rally
le saut en hauteur	high jump
le saut en longueur	long jump
le score	score
le spectateur	spectator
le squash	squash
le tir	shooting
le tir à l'arc	archery
le toboggan	toboggan; water slide, flume
le vol libre	hang-gliding

IMPORTANT WORDS (f)	
la boule	bowl; billiard ball
les boules	bowls
les courses de chevaux	horse-racing
la défense ▷	defence
la piste ▷	ski slope; track
la rencontre ▷	match
la réunion	meeting

USEFUL WORDS (f)	
la balle	(*tennis etc*) ball; bullet
la boxe	boxing
la canne ▷	golf club
la chasse	hunting
la coupe	cup
la course ▷	running; racing; race
une éliminatoire	heat
l'escrime	fencing
une étape	stage; stopping point
la finale	final
la gagnante	winner
la luge ▷	sledge; sledging
la lutte à la corde	tug-of-war
la lutte ▷	wrestling
la mêlée	scrum
la mi-temps (*pl inv*)	half-time
une paire de tennis	pair of tennis *or* gym shoes
la patinoire	ice rink, skating rink
la perdante	loser
la première mi-temps	the first half
la prolongation	extra time
la raquette	(tennis) racket
la réunion hippique	race meeting
la station de sports d'hiver	winter sports resort
la touche ▷	touch
la tribune	stand

ESSENTIAL WORDS (m)

un **acteur** 🕮	actor
le **balcon** ◊	dress circle
le **billet** ◊	ticket
le **cinéma**	cinema
le **cirque** 🕮	circus
le **clown** [klun] 🕮	clown
le **concert**	concert
le **costume** ◊	costume
le **film**	film
le **guichet** ◊ 🕮	box office
le **jeu** ◊ 🕮	acting
un **opéra**	opera
un **orchestre** ◊	orchestra; (seat in the) stalls
le **programme** ◊	programme (*leaflet*)
le **public**	audience
le **rideau** (*pl* -**x**)	curtain
le **spectacle**	show
le **théâtre**	theatre
le **ticket** 🕮	ticket
le **western** 🕮	western

aller au théâtre/au cinéma to go to the theatre/to the cinema
acheter un ticket to buy a ticket
réserver une place to book a seat
un fauteuil d'orchestre a seat in the stalls
mon acteur préféré/mon actrice préférée my favourite actor/actress
jouer to play; **danser** to dance; **chanter** to sing
il a joué le rôle de Rambo he played the part of Rambo
tourner un film to shoot a film

ESSENTIAL WORDS (f)

une **actrice** 📖	actress
l'**ambiance** 📖	atmosphere
une **entrée** ◇	entrance
la **musique**	music
la **pièce** ◇ (**de**	
théâtre) 📖	play
la **place** ◇	seat
la **salle** ◇ 📖	house; audience
la **séance** 📖	performance; showing
la **sortie**	exit, way out
la **vedette** ◇ (*m+f*)	
de cinéma	(film) star

"**prochaine séance: 9 heures**" "next showing: 9 o'clock"
"**version originale**" "in the original language"
"**sous-titré**" "with subtitles"
attendre qn à l'entrée/à la sortie to wait for sb at the entrance/at the exit

---

IMPORTANT WORDS (m)

le ballet 🔲	ballet
le comédien 🔲	actor; comedian
un entracte 🔲	interval
l'espionnage 🔲	spying
le maquillage 🔲	make-up
le pourboire 🔲	tip
le sous-titre 🔲 (*pl* ~s)	sub-title
le titre 🔲	title

USEFUL WORDS (m)

les applaudissements	applause
un auditoire	audience
le cercle dramatique	dramatic society
le décor ◇	scenery
le dramaturge	playwright, dramatist
un écran	screen
le foyer	foyer
le metteur en scène	producer
le parterre ◇	stalls
le personnage	character, person (*in play*)
le poulailler ◇	the "gods"
le producteur	(film) producer
le projecteur	spotlight
le réalisateur	director
le régisseur	stage manager
le rôle	role, part
le scénario	script
le souffleur	prompter
le spectateur	member of the audience
le texte	text; lines
le vestiaire	cloakroom

pendant l'entracte during the interval
offrir un pourboire à l'ouvreuse to give the
  usherette a tip
entrer sur scène to come on stage
jouer le rôle de to play the part of

IMPORTANT WORDS (f)

une **affiche**	notice; poster
la **comédie**	comedy
la **critique**	review; the critics
la **guerre** 📖	war
la **location** ◇ 📖	booking; box office
une **ouvreuse**	usherette
la **réduction**	reduction

USEFUL WORDS (f)

la **corbeille** ◇	circle
les **coulisses**	wings
la **distribution** ◇	cast (*on programme*)
une **estrade**	platform
la **farce**	farce
la **fosse (d'orchestre)**	(orchestra) pit
une **intrigue**	plot
les **jumelles** ◇ de théâtre	opera glasses
la **loge** ◇	box
la **mise en scène**	production
la **pièce à sensation**	thriller
la **rampe**	footlights
la **répétition**	rehearsal
la **répétition générale**	dress rehearsal
la **représentation**	performance
la **scène**	stage; scene
la **tragédie**	tragedy

l'auditoire applaudit the audience applauds
bis! encore!
bravo! bravo!, well done!

ESSENTIAL WORDS (m)

un an	year
un après-midi (pl inv)	afternoon
un instant	moment
le jour	day
le matin	morning
le midi	mid-day, noon
le minuit	midnight
le mois	month
le moment	moment
le quart d'heure	quarter of an hour
le réveil, réveille-matin (pl inv)	alarm clock
le siècle	century; age
le soir	evening
le temps ⟡	time
le week-end (pl ~s)	weekend

à midi at mid-day, at noon
à minuit at midnight
aujourd'hui today
demain tomorrow
hier yesterday
il a 22 ans he is 22 (years old)
j'ai passé l'après-midi à ranger ma chambre I
spent the afternoon tidying up my room
il y a 2 jours 2 days ago
dans 2 jours in 2 days, in 2 days' time
huit jours a week; **quinze jours** a fortnight
tous les jours every day
quel jour sommes-nous? what day is it?
c'est le combien?, le combien sommes-nous?
what's the date?
en ce moment at the moment, at present, just now
3 heures moins le quart a quarter to 3
3 heures et quart a quarter past 3
au 20ème siècle in the 20th century
hier soir last night, yesterday evening

ESSENTIAL WORDS (f)

une année	a (whole) year
une après-midi (*pl inv*)	a (whole) afternoon
une demi-heure (*pl ~s*)	half an hour, a half hour
la fois	time, occasion
une heure	hour
l'heure	time (*in general*)
la journée	(whole) day; daytime
la matinée	(whole) morning
la minute	minute
la montre	watch
la nuit	night
la pendule	clock
la quinzaine	fortnight
la seconde	second
la semaine	week
la soirée	the (whole) evening

l'année dernière/prochaine last/next year
dans une demi-heure in half an hour
une fois/deux fois/trois fois once/twice/three
  times
plusieurs fois several times
3 fois par an 3 times a year
9 fois sur 10 9 times out of 10
il était une fois . . ., il y avait une fois . . . once
  upon a time there was . . .
10 à la fois 10 at one time, 10 at the same time
quelle heure est-il? what time is it?
avez-vous l'heure (exacte *or* **juste)?** have you got
  the (right) time?
**il est 6 heures/6 heures moins 10/6 heures et
  demie** it is 6 o'clock/10 to 6/half past 6
tout à l'heure (*past*) a short while ago; (*future*)
  soon, shortly
tôt, de bonne heure early; **tard** late
cette nuit (*already past*) last night; (*still to come*)
  tonight

IMPORTANT WORDS (m)

l'avenir	future
le lendemain	the next day, the day after
le retard	delay; lateness
le surlendemain	two days later, the day after next

USEFUL WORDS (m)

le cadran	face (of clock etc), dial
le calendrier	calendar
le chronomètre	stopwatch
le futur	future; the future tense
un intervalle	interval (of time)
le passé	the past; the past tense
le présent	present (time); present tense

---

après-demain the day after tomorrow
avant-hier the day before yesterday
à l'avenir in (the) future
être en retard to be late
le jour de congé day off, holiday
le jour férié public holiday, bank holiday
le jour ouvrable week-day
par un jour de pluie on a rainy day, one rainy day
au lever du jour at dawn, at daybreak
le lendemain matin/soir the following morning/ evening
à présent at present, now; nowadays
vous êtes en retard you are late
cette montre avance/retarde this watch is fast/ slow
le cours du soir evening class
il passe tout son temps à travailler he spends all his time working
arriver à temps, arriver à l'heure to arrive on time
pour combien de temps ...? how long ...?

IMPORTANT WORDS (f)	
l'horloge	(large) clock
la veille	the day before, the eve (of sth)

USEFUL WORDS (f)	
une aiguille ◇	hand (of clock etc)
une année bissextile	leap year
l'avant-veille (pl ~s)	two days before or previously
la décennie	decade
une époque	epoch; (particular) time
une horloge normande	grandfather clock
la pendule à coucou	cuckoo clock

avancer/retarder l'horloge to put the clock(s) forward/back
faire la grasse matinée to have a long lie, have a lie-in
d'une minute à l'autre any minute now
aujourd'hui en huit a week today
la veille de Noël (on) Christmas Eve
la veille au soir the previous evening, the night before
à cette époque(-là) at that time, in those days

ESSENTIAL WORDS (m)	
le bricolage	D.I.Y., do-it-yourself
le bricoleur	home handyman

IMPORTANT WORDS (m)	
un atelier	workshop
le machin	thing, contraption
un ouvre-boîte(s) (pl inv)	tin opener
le tire-bouchon (pl ~s)	corkscrew

USEFUL WORDS (m)	
le cadenas	padlock
le chantier	construction site
le ciseau (pl -x)	chisel
les ciseaux	scissors
le clou	nail
l'échafaudage	scaffolding
un élastique	rubber band, elastic band
un escabeau (pl -x)	stepladder, pair of steps
le fil de fer (barbelé)	(barbed) wire
le foret	drill
le marteau (pl -x)	hammer
le marteau-piqueur	pneumatic drill
un outil	tool
le pic ◇	pick, pickaxe
le pinceau (pl -x)	paintbrush
le ressort	spring
le scotch	sellotape, adhesive tape
le tournevis	screwdriver

faire du bricolage to do odd jobs
enfoncer un clou to hammer in a nail
"attention à la peinture!", "peinture fraîche" "wet paint"
peindre to paint; **tapisser** to wallpaper
"chantier interdit" "construction site: keep out"

ESSENTIAL WORDS (f)	
la clé, clef	key
la corde ⇨	rope
la machine	machine

IMPORTANT WORDS (f)	
la serrure 🗎	lock

USEFUL WORDS (f)	
une aiguille ⇨	needle
la bêche	spade
la boîte à outils	toolbox
la boîte à ouvrage	workbox
la clef anglaise	spanner
la colle ⇨	glue
une échelle	ladder
la fourche	(garden) fork
la lime	file
la pelle ⇨	shovel
la perceuse	drill
la pile	battery
les pinces	pliers
la pioche	pick, pickaxe
la planche	plank
la punaise ⇨	drawing pin, thumbtack
la scie	saw
la vis [vis]	screw

utile useful; **inutile** useless
pratique handy
casser to break; **couper** to cut; **réparer** to mend
fermer à clé to lock
fixer avec une vis to screw (in); **dévisser** to
  unscrew

ESSENTIAL WORDS (*m*)

un **agent** (de police)	policeman
un **arrêt** (de bus)	bus stop
le **bâtiment**	building
le **bureau** 🕮 (*pl* -**x**) de **poste**	post office
le **bureau** ▷ (*pl* -**x**)	office
le **centre-ville** (*pl* ~s~s)	town centre
le **cinéma**	cinema
le **coin**	corner
le **commissariat** de **police**	police station
le **département**	*like British "region"*
les **environs**	surroundings, outskirts
l'**habitant**	inhabitant
le :**HLM** 🕮 (**habitation à loyer modéré**)	council flat *or* house
l'**hôtel de ville**	town hall
l'**hôtel** ▷	hotel; mansion
un **immeuble**	block of flats
le **jardin public**	public park
le **magasin**	shop
le **marché** ▷	market
le **métro**	underground
le **musée** 🕮	museum; art gallery
le **parc**	park
le **parking** ▷	car park
le **piéton**	pedestrian
le **pont** ▷	bridge
le **quartier**	district
le **restaurant**	restaurant
le **syndicat d'initiative, SI**	tourist information office
le **taxi**	taxi
le **théâtre**	theatre
le **tour** ▷	tour
le **touriste**	tourist
le **véhicule** 🕮	vehicle

ESSENTIAL WORDS (f)

une **auto**	car
la **banlieue**	suburbs
la **banque**	bank
la **boutique** 📖	(small) shop
la **cathédrale**	cathedral
une **église**	church
la **gare**	(train) station
la **gare routière**	coach station
la **:HLM** 📖 (habitation	
à loyer modéré)	council flat *or* house
la **mairie**	town hall
la **piscine**	swimming pool
la **place** ◇	square
la **police**	police
la **pollution** 📖	air pollution
la **poste** ◇	post office
la **route**	road
la **rue**	street
la **station de taxis**	taxi stand *or* rank
la **station-service**	
(*pl* ~s~)	service station, garage
la **tour** ◇	tower
une **usine**	factory
la **ville**	town, city
la **voiture** ◇	car
la **vue** 📖	view

je vais en ville I'm going into town
au centre-ville in the town centre
sur la place in the square
une rue à sens unique a one-way street
traverser la rue to cross the street
au coin de la rue at the corner of the street
habiter la banlieue to live in the suburbs

IMPORTANT WORDS (*m*)

le carnet ⇨ (de tickets)	book of tickets
le carrefour	crossroads
le château (*pl* -x)	castle
un embouteillage 📖	traffic jam
un endroit	place
le jardin zoologique	zoo
le kiosque (à journaux)	(newspaper) stall
le lieu (*pl* -x)	place
le maire	mayor
le monument	monument
le passant	passer-by
le sens unique 📖	one-way street
le trottoir	pavement

marcher to walk
prendre le bus/le métro *etc* to take the bus/the underground *etc*
acheter un carnet de tickets to buy a book of tickets

IMPORTANT WORDS (f)

une affiche	notice; poster
la bibliothèque ⇨	library
la chaussée	roadway
la circulation	traffic
la rue principale	main street

circuler to move (along)
visiter la ville to go sight-seeing (*in the town*)
regarder un plan de la ville to look at a map of the
   town
industriel(le) industrial; **historique** historic
joli(e) pretty; **laid(e)** ugly
propre clean; **sale** dirty

USEFUL WORDS (m)	
un abribus	bus shelter
un arrondissement	district
un autobus à/sans impériale	double/single-decker bus
le bistrot	café
le cimetière	cemetery, graveyard
le citadin	town dweller
le citoyen	citizen
le comté	county
le conseil municipal	town council
le défilé	procession, parade
le dépliant	leaflet
un édifice	building
un égout	sewer
le faubourg	suburb
le gratte-ciel (pl inv)	skyscraper
le panneau (pl -x)	roadsign
le passage clouté	pedestrian crossing
le pavé	cobblestone; paving
le refuge	traffic island
le réverbère	street lamp
les signaux routiers	roadsigns
le sondage d'opinion	opinion poll
le square	square (with gardens)
le tournant, le virage	turning, bend

USEFUL WORDS (f)	
une **agglomération**	built-up area
la **bousculade**	bustle, crush
la **camionnette de livraison**	delivery van
la **caserne de pompiers**	fire station
la **cité**	city (*old part*)
la **cité universitaire**	university halls of residence
les **curiosités**	sights, places of interest
la **flèche**	spire; arrow
la **foule**	crowd
la **galerie** ⟡	art gallery
la **grand'route**	main road
la **grand-rue**	main street
une **impasse**	dead end
la **piste cyclable**	cycle path
la **population**	population
la **prison**	prison
la **queue** ⟡ [kø]	queue
la **statue**	statue
la **voiture d'enfant**	pram

ESSENTIAL WORDS (*m*)	
un aller-retour	return ticket
un aller-simple	single ticket
les bagages	luggage
le billet ◇	ticket
le buffet◇	station buffet
le carnet ◇	book of tickets
le compartiment ⌂	compartment
le départ ⌂	departure
le douanier ⌂	customs officer
un express ⌂	fast train
le frein ⌂	brake
le guichet ◇ ⌂	booking *or* ticket office
l'horaire ⌂	timetable
le mécanicien ◇ ⌂	engine-driver
le métro	underground (railway)
le numéro	number
les objets trouvés	lost and found
le passeport	passport
le plan ◇	plan, map
le pont ◇	bridge
le porteur	porter
le prix du billet	fare
le prix du ticket	fare
le quai ◇ [ke]	platform
le rapide ⌂	express train
les renseignements ◇	information
le retard	delay
le sac	bag
le supplément ⌂	extra charge
le taxi	taxi
le ticket ⌂	ticket
le train	train
le train express ⌂	fast train
le train rapide ⌂	express train
le vélo ◇	bike
le voyage	journey
le voyageur ⌂	traveller

ESSENTIAL WORDS (f)

une **arrivée** 🔲	arrival
la **bicyclette** 🔲	bicycle
la **classe** 🔲	class
la **consigne**	left-luggage office
la **consigne**	
automatique 🔲	left-luggage locker
la **correspondance** 🔲	connection
la **direction** 🔲	direction
la **douane** 🔲	customs
une **entrée** ◊	entrance
la **gare**	station
la **ligne** 🔲	line, track
la **place** ◊	seat
la **réduction**	reduction
la **réservation** 🔲	reservation, booking
la **salle d'attente**	waiting room
la **sortie**	exit
la **station**	underground *or* subway
(de métro)	station
la **station (de taxis)**	taxi stand *or* rank
la **valise**	case, suitcase
la **voie** ◊ 🔲	track, line
la **voiture** ◊	carriage, coach

demander des renseignements to ask for
information
réserver une place to book a seat
payer un supplément to pay an extra charge
faire/défaire ses bagages to pack/unpack (one's
luggage)
j'aime voyager par le train I like travelling by train
prendre le train to take *or* catch the train
manquer le train to miss the train
monter dans le train/bus to get into the train/onto
the bus
descendre du train/bus to get off the train/bus
c'est pris?/libre? is this seat taken?/free?

IMPORTANT WORDS (m)	
le chemin de fer 🗀	railway
le conducteur 🗀	(train-)driver
un escalier roulant 🗀	escalator
un omnibus	slow train
le pourboire 🗀	tip
le tarif 🗀	rate, fare
le train omnibus	slow train
le wagon-lit (*pl* ~s~s)	sleeping car
le wagon-restaurant	
(*pl* ~s~s)	dining car

USEFUL WORDS (m)	
le chauffeur ◊	fireman, stoker
le chef de gare	stationmaster
le chef de train	guard
le cheminot	railwayman
le contrôleur	ticket collector
le coup de sifflet	blast on whistle
le déraillement	derailment
le filet ◊	luggage rack
le fourgon du chef de	
train	guard's van
un indicateur	timetable
le passage à niveau	level crossing
les rails	rails
le signal d'alarme	alarm, communication
	cord
le train de	
marchandises	goods train
le trajet	journey
le wagon	carriage, coach

le train est en retard the train is late
un compartiment fumeur/non-fumeur a smoking/
non-smoking compartment
"défense de se pencher au dehors" "do not lean
out of the window"

IMPORTANT WORDS (f)	
la barrière ▷	barrier
la couchette	couchette, sleeping car
la destination	destination
la durée	length, duration
la frontière	border, frontier
l'horloge	(large) clock
la portière	(carriage) door
la section ⌷	fare stage (*on bus*)
la SNCF	French Railways

USEFUL WORDS (f)	
la banquette	seat
la carte d'abonnement	season ticket
une étiquette	label
la locomotive	locomotive, engine
la malle	trunk
la salle des pas perdus	waiting room
la sonnette d'alarme	alarm, communication cord
la voie ferrée	(railway) line *or* track

je t'accompagnerai à la gare I'll go to the station with you

je viendrai te chercher à la gare I'll come and fetch you from the station

je passerai te prendre à la gare I'll come and pick you up at the station

le train de 10 heures à destination de Paris/en provenance de Paris the 10 o'clock train to Paris/ from Paris

ESSENTIAL WORDS (m)

un arbre	tree
un arbre de Noël	Christmas tree
le bois 🕮	wood

USEFUL WORDS (m)

un arbre fruitier	fruit tree
le bouleau (*pl* **-x**)	birch
le bourgeon	bud
le buis	box tree
le buisson	bush
le châtaignier	chestnut tree
le chêne	oak
un érable	maple
le feuillage	leaves, foliage
le frêne	ash
le :hêtre	beech
le :hêtre rouge	copper beech
le :houx	holly
un if	yew
le marronnier	(horse) chestnut tree
un orme	elm
le peuplier	poplar
le pin	pine
le platane	plane tree
le rameau (*pl* **-x**)	branch
le sapin	fir tree
le saule (pleureur)	(weeping) willow
le tilleul	lime tree
le tronc	trunk
le verger	orchard
le vignoble	vineyard

une chaise de *or* **en bois** a wooden chair
à l'ombre d'un arbre in the shade of a tree

ESSENTIAL WORDS (f)	
la branche	branch
la feuille	leaf

IMPORTANT WORDS (f)	
la forêt	forest

USEFUL WORDS (f)	
une aubépine	hawthorn
la baie ◇	berry
l'écorce	bark
la racine	root

les feuilles jaunissent en automne the leaves turn yellow in autumn

ESSENTIAL WORDS (m)	
le chou 📖 *(pl* **-x)**	cabbage
le chou-fleur 📖	
(pl **~x~s)**	cauliflower
le :haricot	bean
le :haricot vert	French bean
les légumes	vegetables
les petits pois	(garden) peas

IMPORTANT WORDS (m)	
le champignon 📖	mushroom
un oignon [ɔɲɔ] 📖	onion

USEFUL WORDS (m)	
l'ail [aj]	garlic
un artichaut	artichoke
le céléri	celery
le chou *(pl* **-x)** **de**	
Bruxelles	Brussels sprout
le concombre	cucumber
le cresson	cress
un épi de maïs [ma-is]	corn on the cob
les épinards	spinach
le navet	turnip
le persil [pɛrsi]	parsley
le piment doux	(sweet) pepper
le poireau *(pl* **-x)**	leek
le poivron	(sweet) pepper
le radis	radish

aimer to like; **détester** to hate; **préférer** to prefer
cultiver des légumes to grow vegetables
saucisson à l'ail garlic sausage

ESSENTIAL WORDS (f)
---

la carotte 📖	carrot
les crudités 📖	*selection of salads*
la pomme de terre	
(*pl* **~s de terre)**	potato
la salade (verte)	(green) salad
la tomate	tomato; tomato plant

USEFUL WORDS (f)
---

les asperges	asparagus
une aubergine	aubergine
la betterave	beetroot
la chicorée	endive
la courge	marrow
la courgette	courgette
une endive	chicory
la laitue	lettuce

carottes râpées grated carrot
choucroute garnie sauerkraut with meat
pommes persillées potatoes with parsley
pommes frites chips; **pommes vapeur** boiled
    potatoes
rouge comme une tomate as red as a beetroot
organique organic
végétarien(ne) vegetarian

ESSENTIAL WORDS (m)

un autobus	bus
un autocar 📖	coach
un avion	plane, aeroplane
le bateau (*pl* **-x**)	boat
le bus	bus
le camion	lorry, truck
le car	coach
le casque 📖	helmet
le ferry	ferry
le métro	underground
le moyen de transport	means of transport
le prix du billet	fare (*any mode of transport*)
le prix du ticket	fare (*boat, plane*)
le scooter 📖	scooter
le taxi	taxi
le train	train
le véhicule 📖	vehicle
le vélo ♢	bike
le vélomoteur	moped

IMPORTANT WORDS (m)

l'arrière 📖	back
l'avant 📖	front
le ballon ♢	balloon
le bateau à rames/à voiles	rowing/sailing boat
l'hélicoptère	helicopter
l'hovercraft	hovercraft
le poids lourd 📖	heavy lorry, juggernaut
le risque	risk

voyager to travel
il est allé à Paris en avion he went to Paris by air, he flew to Paris
prendre le bus/le métro/le train to take the bus/ the metro/the train

---
ESSENTIAL WORDS (f)
---

la bicyclette 📖	bicycle
la camionnette	(small) van
la caravane	caravan
la distance 📖	distance
la moto, motocyclette	motorbike, motorcycle
la voiture ◇	car; coach, carriage

IMPORTANT WORDS (f)
---

une ambulance	ambulance
la voiture de dépannage	breakdown van
la voiture de pompiers	fire engine

faire de la bicyclette to go cycling
appelez l'ambulance! call an ambulance!
on peut y aller en voiture we can go there by car *or* in the car
conduire une voiture to drive (a car)
une promenade en voiture a drive
une voiture de location a hired *or* rented car
une voiture de sport a sports car
une voiture de course a racing car
une voiture de fonction a company car
"voitures d'occasion" "second-hand cars"
les transports en commun public transport

USEFUL WORDS (m)	
un aéroglisseur	hovercraft
un astronef	spaceship
le bac ◇	ferry(-boat)
le bateau-mouche	
(*pl* **x- s**)	*tour boat on the Seine*
le break [bʀɛk]	estate car
le bulldozer	
[buldozœʀ]	bulldozer
le camion-citerne	
(*pl* **s- s**)	tanker
le canoë [kanɔe]	canoe
le canot	rowing boat
le canot de sauvetage	lifeboat
le char (d'assaut)	tank
le cyclomoteur	moped
le dirigeable	airship
le funiculaire	funicular (railway)
l'hydravion	seaplane
le navire	ship
un OVNI (objet volant	UFO, unidentified flying
non identifié)	object
le paquebot	passenger steamer, liner
le pétrolier	oil tanker (*ship*)
le planeur	glider
le porte-avions	
(*pl inv*)	aircraft carrier
le remorqueur	tug, tugboat
le semi-remorque	
(*pl* **- s**)	articulated lorry
le sous-marin (*pl* **- s**)	submarine
le téléphérique	cable car
le télésiège	chairlift
le tramway	tram
le vaisseau (*pl* **-x**)	vessel
le vapeur ◇	steamer
le yacht [jɔt]	yacht

USEFUL WORDS (f)

la camionnette de livraison	delivery van
la charrette	cart
la fusée	rocket
la jeep	jeep
la locomotive	engine, locomotive
la mobylette	moped
la péniche	barge
la remorque	trailer
la soucoupe volante	flying saucer
la vedette ▷	speedboat
la voiture d'enfant	pram
la voiture pie	Panda car

ESSENTIAL WORDS (m)

l'air ⇨	air
un an	year
un après-midi (*pl inv*)	afternoon
l'automne	autumn
le brouillard	fog
le bulletin de la météo	weather report
le ciel ▢	sky
le climat ▢	climate
le degré ▢	degree
l'est	east
l'été	summer
le froid	cold
l'hiver	winter
le matin	morning
le mois	month
le monde ▢	world
le nord	north
le nuage ▢	cloud
l'ouest	west
le parapluie ▢	umbrella
le pays ⇨	country
le printemps	spring
le soir	evening
le soleil ⇨	sun; sunshine
le sud	south
le temps ⇨	weather
le vent	wind

quel temps fait-il? what's the weather like?
il fait chaud/froid it's hot/cold
il fait beau it's a lovely day
il fait mauvais (temps) it's a horrible day
il fait du soleil/du vent it's sunny/windy
en plein air in the open air
il fait du brouillard it's foggy

ESSENTIAL WORDS (f)	

une **après-midi** (*pl inv*)	afternoon
la **glace** ◇	ice
une **île**	island
la **journée**	(whole) day; daytime
la **lumière** ▭	light
la **météo** ▭	(weather) forecast
la **montagne** ▭	mountain
la **neige**	snow
la **nuit**	night
la **pluie**	rain
la **région**	region, area
la **saison** ▭	season
la **température**	temperature

écouter la météo *or* **les prévisions** to listen to the forecast
pleuvoir to rain; **neiger** to snow
il pleut it's raining; **il neige** it's snowing
le soleil brille the sun is shining
le vent souffle the wind is blowing
il gèle it's freezing
geler to freeze; **fondre** to melt
ensoleillé sunny
neigeux(euse) snowy
orageux(euse) stormy
pluvieux(euse) rainy, wet
frais (fraîche) cool
variable changeable
humide humid; damp
mouillé(e) wet
le ciel est nuageux/couvert the sky is cloudy/ overcast

IMPORTANT WORDS (m)	
le changement	change
le coucher du soleil	sunset
l'endroit	place
le lever du soleil	sunrise
un orage	thunderstorm

USEFUL WORDS (m)	
un amoncellement de neige	snowdrift
un arc-en-ciel (pl ~s~~)	rainbow
le baromètre	barometer
le chasse-neige (pl inv)	snowplough
le clair de lune	moonlight
le coup de tonnerre	thunderclap
le coup de vent	gust of wind
le courant d'air	draught
le crépuscule	twilight
les dégâts	damage, destruction
le dégel	thaw
le déluge	downpour
un éclair	flash of lightning
le flocon de neige	snowflake
le gel	frost
le givre	frost
le glaçon ⬦	icicle
un ouragan	hurricane
le paratonnerre	lightning conductor
le point de congélation	freezing point
le rayon ⬦ **(de soleil)**	ray (of sunshine)
le smog	smog
le tonnerre	thunder
le tremblement de terre	earthquake
le verglas	black ice

IMPORTANT WORDS (f)

une amélioration ▭	improvement
une averse ▭	shower
la chaleur	heat
la côte ◇	coast
une éclaircie ▭	bright period
une étoile ▭	star
la fumée	smoke
la poussière	dust
la précipitation ▭	rainfall
les prévisions (météorologiques)	(weather) forecast
la tempête ▭	tempest, gale, storm
la visibilité ▭	visibility

USEFUL WORDS (f)

l'atmosphère	atmosphere
l'aube	dawn
la brise	breeze
la brume ▭	mist
la canicule	heatwave
la chute de neige	snowfall
la congère	snowdrift
la flaque d'eau	puddle
les fleurs de givre	frost patterns (*on window*)
la foudre	lightning
la gelée ◇	frost
la goutte de pluie	raindrop
la grêle	hail
une inondation	flood
la lune	moon
l'obscurité	darkness
une ombre	shadow
la rafale	squall
la rosée	dew
la sécheresse	drought
les ténèbres	darkness
la vague de chaleur	heatwave

ESSENTIAL WORDS (m)

le bureau ◇ (pl -x)	office
le dîner	dinner
le dortoir ▭	dormitory
le drap ◇ ▭	sheet
le garçon ◇	boy
le lit	bed
le petit déjeuner	breakfast
le repas	meal
le séjour ▭	stay
le silence ▭	silence
le tarif ▭	rate(s)
le visiteur ▭	visitor
les W.-C. ▭	toilet(s)

IMPORTANT WORDS (m)

le guide	guide-book
le linge ◇	bedclothes, bedding; washing
le règlement	rule
le repas préparé	prepared meal
le sac à dos	backpack, rucksack
le sac de couchage	sleeping bag

je voudrais louer un sac de couchage I would like to hire a sleeping bag

---

ESSENTIAL WORDS (f)

une auberge de
   jeunesse   youth hostel
  la carte ▷   map; card
  la cuisine ▷   kitchen; cooking
  la douche   shower
  la fille   girl
  la nuit   night
  la place ▷   room; place
  la poubelle   dustbin
  la salle à manger dining room
  la salle de bains   bathroom
  la salle de jeux ▭ games room
  les toilettes   toilet(s)
  les vacances   holidays

IMPORTANT WORDS (f)

  la carte d'adhérent membership card
  la randonnée ▭   walk; hike; drive

passer une nuit à l'auberge de jeunesse to spend
  a night at the youth hostel

The vocabulary items on pages 204 to 236 have been grouped under parts of speech rather than topics because they can apply in a wide range of circumstances. You should learn to use them just as freely as the vocabulary already given.

CONJUNCTIONS

CONJUNCTIONS

alors que when, as, while
aussi so, therefore
aussi . . . que as . . . as
avant de + *infinitive* before
car for, because
cependant however
c'est-à-dire that is to say
comme as
comment how
depuis que (ever) since
dès que as soon as
donc so; then
et and
et alors? so what!
et lui? what about him?
lorsque when, as
maintenant que now (that)
mais but
mais non! of course not!

au moment où (just) as
ne . . . que only
ni . . . ni neither . . . nor
or now
ou or
ou . . . ou either . . . or
ou bien or (else)
parce que because
pendant que while
pourquoi why
pourvu que + *subj* provided that, so long as
puisque since, because
quand when
que that; than
si if
sinon otherwise; other than, except
tandis que whilst
tant que so long as, while
vu que seeing (that); in view of the fact that

ADJECTIVES

abordable within reach
abrégé(e) shortened
absurde absurd
actif, active active
actuel(le) present (*time*)
aérien(ne) aerial
affectueux, -euse affectionate
affreux, -euse frightful
âgé(e) old
agité restless; busy (*street*); stormy (*sea*)
agréable pleasant
agricole agricultural
aigu, aiguë acute; piercing
aimable kind, nice
aîné(e) elder, eldest
amer, amère bitter
amusant(e) amusing, enjoyable
ancien(ne) old, former
animé(e) busy, crowded
annuel(le) annual
anonyme anonymous
anxieux, -euse anxious, worried
appliqué(e) diligent ɪ
apte capable
arrière: siège *m* **arrière** back seat
assis(e) sitting, seated
aucun(e) any, no, not any
automatique automatic
autre other
avant: siège *m* **avant** front seat
barbu bearded
bas(se) low
beau (bel), belle beautiful, fine
bête silly
bien fine, well; comfortable
bienvenu(e) welcome
bizarre strange, odd
blessé(e) injured
bon(ne) good
bon marché *inv* cheap
bordé(e) de lined with
bouillant(e) boiling
bouleversé(e) thrown into confusion
brave fine, good
bref, brève brief
brillant(e) bright, brilliant; shiny
bruyant(e) noisy
calme calm
capable capable
carré(e) square
célèbre famous
certain(e) sure, certain
chaque each, every
chargé(e) de loaded with; responsible for
charmant(e) delightful
chaud(e) warm; hot; *see* **avoir, faire**
cher, chère dear; expensive
chic smart
choquant(e) shocking

chouette great, brilliant
clair(e) clear; light
classique classical
climatisé(e) air-conditioned
commode convenient
complet, complète complete; full
compliqué(e) complicated
composé(e) de comprising
compris(e) understood; including
confortable comfortable
contemporain(e) contemporary
content(e) happy
continuel(le) continuing
convenable suitable
correct(e) correct
couché(e) lying down
courageux, -euse courageous
court(e) short
couvert(e) de covered with
créé(e) created, established
cruel(le) cruel
cuit(e) cooked; **bien cuit** well done (*of steak*)
culturel(le) cultural
curieux, -euse curious, strange
dangereux, -euse dangerous
debout standing (up)
décevant(e) disappointing
déchiré(e) torn
découragé(e) discouraged
déçu(e) disappointed

dégoûté(e) disgusted
délicat(e) delicate
délicieux, -ieuse delicious
dernier, dernière last, latest
désagréable unpleasant
désert(e) deserted
désespéré(e) desperate
désolé(e) desolate; sorry
détestable foul, ghastly
détruit(e) destroyed
différent(e) different
difficile difficult
digne worthy
direct(e) direct
disponible available
distingué(e) distinguished
distrait(e) absent-minded
divers(e) different
divertissant(e) entertaining
divin(e) divine
divisé(e) divided
doré(e) golden; gilt
doux, douce gentle; sweet; soft
droit(e) straight; right(hand)
drôle funny
dur(e) hard
éclairé(e): bien éclairé(e) well lit
économique economic; economical
effrayé(e) frightened
égal(e) equal; even;

steady
électrique electric
élégant(e) elegant
élevé(e) high; **bien élevé(e)** well-mannered
embêtant(e) annoying
enchanté(e) delighted
ennuyé(e) bothered; annoyed
ennuyeux, -euse boring
énorme huge
ensoleillé(e) sunny
entendu(e) agreed; **bien entendu** of course
entier, entière whole
épais(se) thick
épouvantable terrible
épuisé(e) exhausted, worn out
essentiel(le) essential
essoufflé(e) out of breath
étendu(e) stretched out
étonnant(e) astonishing
étonné(e) astonished; **d'un air étonné** in astonishment
étrange strange
étranger, étrangère foreign
étroit(e) narrow; strict
éveillé(e) awake
évident(e) evident, obvious
exact(e) exact
excellent(e) excellent
expérimenté(e) experienced
extraordinaire extraordinary
fâché(e) angry
facile easy
faible weak; faint
fatigant(e) tiring
fatigué(e) tired
faux, fausse false, wrong
favori(te) favourite
fermé(e) closed, shut; off (of tap etc)
féroce fierce
fier, fière proud
fin(e) fine; thin
final(e) final
fondé(e) founded
formidable tremendous, magnificent; great
fort(e) strong; hard
fou, folle mad; **un succès fou** a great success
fragile fragile; frail
frais, fraîche fresh, cool
froid(e) cold; see **avoir, faire**
furieux, -euse furious
futur(e) future; **future maman** f mother-to-be
gai(e) gay
gauche left(hand)
général(e) general
gentil(le) kind, nice
gonflé(e) blown up
gracieux, -ieuse graceful
grand(e) big, great; tall; high
gratuit(e) free
grave serious
gros(se) big; fat

habile skilful
habitué(e) à used to
habituel(le) usual
haut(e) high; tall
heureux, -euse happy
historique historic(al)
honnête honest
identique identical
illuminé(e) lit; floodlit
illustré(e) illustrated
imaginaire imaginary
immense huge, immense
immobile still, motionless
important(e) important
impossible impossible
impressionnant(e) impressive
imprévu(e) unforeseen
inattendu(e) unexpected
incapable (de) incapable (of)
inconnu(e) unknown
incroyable unbelievable
indispensable indispensable
industriel(le) industrial
inondé(e) flooded
inquiet, inquiète anxious, worried
insouciant(e) carefree
insupportable horrid, unbearable
intelligent(e) intelligent
interdit(e) prohibited
intéressant(e) interesting
interminable endless
interrompu(e) interrupted
inutile useless
irrité(e) annoyed
isolé(e) isolated
jaloux, -ouse jealous
jeune young
joli(e) pretty
joyeux, -euse merry, cheerful
juste just; correct
lâche cowardly
laid(e) ugly
large wide; broad
léger, légère light
lent(e) slow
leur/leurs their
libre free, vacant
local(e) local
long(ue) long
lourd(e) heavy
de luxe luxurious, luxury
magique magic; magical
magnifique magnificent
maigre thin
malade ill
malheureux, -euse unhappy, unfortunate
malhonnête dishonest
mauvais(e) bad; **à la mauvaise ligne** on the wrong line; **de mauvaise humeur** in a bad temper
mécanique mechanical
méchant(e) naughty
mécontent(e) unhappy
médical(e) medical
meilleur(e) better, best
même same
merveilleux, -euse

marvellous
militaire military
minable pathetic, pitiful
mince slim, slender
mobile mobile; moving;
  movable
moche ugly; rotten, bad
moderne modern
moindre least
mon/ma/mes my
montagneux, -euse
  mountainous
mort(e) dead
mouillé(e) wet through
mouvementé(e) lively
moyen(ne) average
mû, mue (par) moved
  (by)
multicolore
  multicoloured
muni(e) de provided with
municipal(e) municipal,
  town
mûr(e) ripe
musclé(e) muscular,
  brawny
musical(e) musical
mystérieux, -euse
  mysterious
natal(e) native
national(e) national
naturel(le) natural
né(e) born
nécessaire necessary
nerveux, -euse nervous
net(te) clear, sharp
neuf, neuve new;
  tout(e) neuf (neuve)
  brand new

nombreux, -euse
  numerous
normal(e) normal
notre/nos our
**nouveau (nouvel),
  nouvelle** new
noyé(e) drowned
nul: match nul draw
obligatoire compulsory
obligé(e) de obliged to
occupé(e) engaged,
  taken (*of room*); busy
  (*of person*); engaged (*of
  phone*)
officiel(le) official
ordinaire ordinary
original(e) original
orné(e) de decorated
  with
outré(e) outraged,
  appalled
ouvert(e) open; on (*of
  tap etc*)
paisible peaceful
pâle pale
pareil(le) similar, same;
  une somme pareille
  such a sum
paresseux, -euse lazy
parfait(e) perfect
particulier, particulière
  particular; private
passionnant(e) exciting
passionné(e) passionate
patient(e) patient
pauvre poor
pénible painful
permanent(e)
  permanent

perpétuel(le) perpetual
personnel(le) personal
petit(e) small, little
pittoresque picturesque
plat(e) flat
plein(e) (de) full (of); **en plein air** in the open air; **en plein jour** in broad daylight
plusieurs several
pneumatique inflatable
poli(e) polite; polished
populaire popular
portatif, -ive portable
possible possible
pratique practical; handy
précédent(e) previous
précieux, -euse precious
précis(e) precise; **à cinq heures précises** at exactly five o'clock
préféré(e) favourite
premier, première first
pressant(e) urgent
pressé(e): être pressé(e) to be in a hurry
prêt(e) ready; **prêt à porter** ready to wear, off-the-peg
primaire primary
privé(e) private
privilégié(e) privileged
prochain(e) next
proche nearby; close
profond(e) deep
propre own; clean
prudent(e) cautious
public, publique public
publicitaire publicity

quel(le) what
quelque(s) some
rafraîchissant(e) refreshing
rangé(e): bien rangé(e) neat and tidy
rapide fast, quick, rapid
rare rare
ravi(e) delighted
récent(e) recent
reconnaissant(e) grateful
rectangulaire rectangular
religieux, -euse religious
réservé(e) reserved
responsable (de) responsible (for)
rêveur, -euse dreamy
riche rich, wealthy
ridicule ridiculous
rond(e) round
roulé(e) rolled up
rusé(e) cunning
sage good, well-behaved; wise
sain et sauf safe and sound
sale dirty; **un sale temps** terrible weather
sanitaire sanitary
satisfait(e) (de) satisfied (with)
sauvage uncivilized; wild
scolaire school (*year etc*)
sec, sèche dry
second(e) second
secondaire secondary
secret, secrète secret
sensass great, fantastic
sensationel(le) sensational
sérieux, -euse serious

serré(e) tight, close
seul(e) alone; lonely; single
sévère severe, strict
simple simple, plain
sincère sincere
sinistre sinister
situé(e) situated
social(e) social
solennel(le) solemn
solide solid
sombre dark
son/sa/ses his, her, its, one's
peu soucieux (soucieuse) unconcerned
soudain(e) sudden
soupçonneux, -euse suspicious
souriant(e) smiling
sous-marin(e) underwater
spécial(e) special
suivant(e) following
suivi(e) de followed by
super super, great
superbe magnificent
supérieur(e) upper; advanced
supplémentaire extra
sûr(e) sure
surprenant(e) surprising
sympa(thique) likeable
technique technical

tel(le) such
temporaire temporary
terrible terrible; great
théâtral(e) theatrical
timide shy
ton/ta/tes your
touristique tourist (*area etc*)
tout/toute/toutes all
traditionnel(le) traditional
tranquille quiet, peaceful
trempé(e) soaked
triste sad
troublé(e) disturbed
typique typical
uni(e) plain
unique only (*hope etc*); unique
urbain(e) urban
urgent(e) urgent
utile useful
varié(e) varied; various
vaste vast
véritable real, genuine
vide empty
vieux (vieil), vieille old
vif, vive keen; vivid; bright
vilain(e) naughty; ugly; nasty
violent(e) violent
vivant(e) alive; lively
voisin(e) neighbouring
votre/vos your
vrai(e) true

ADVERBS AND PREPOSITIONS

à to, at
d'abord first, at first
tout d'abord first of all
aux abords de alongside
absolument absolutely
actuellement at present
admirablement
 admirably
afin de so as to
ailleurs elsewhere
d'ailleurs moreover
ainsi thus
ainsi que as well as
alors then; while
anxieusement anxiously
après after
après-demain the day
 after tomorrow
d'après according to
assez fairly, quite
assez de enough
aujourd'hui today
auparavant previously
auprès de by, close to,
 next to
aussi also, too; as
aussitôt at once
autant (de) as much; as
 many
d'autant plus (que) all
 the more (since)
autour (de) around
autrefois formerly
autrement otherwise,
 differently
autrement dit in other
 words

autrement que other
 than
à l'avance in advance
avant (de) before
avec with
en bas downstairs, at the
 bottom
beaucoup a lot; much,
 far
beaucoup de a lot of;
 many
bien well
bien entendu of course
bientôt soon
à bord (de) on board
au bord de beside
au bout de after (of
 time); at the end of
bref "to cut a long story
 short"
brusquement abruptly,
 sharply
cependant however
certainement certainly
sans cesse without
 stopping, unceasingly
chez at (or to) the house
 of
chez moi/toi/lui/elle at
 my/your/his/her house
combien (de) how much,
 how many
comme as, like
comme d'habitude as
 usual
comme toujours as
 usual

comment? how?
complètement completely
y compris including
par conséquent as a result
continuellement continually
contre against
ci-contre opposite (this)
par contre on the other hand
à côté de next to, beside
de ce côté (de) on this side (of)
de l'autre côté (de) on the other side (of)
juste à côté next door
couramment fluently
dans in, into
davantage (de) more
de of, from
debout standing
dedans inside
(au) dehors outside
déjà already
demain tomorrow
après-demain the day after tomorrow
depuis since, for
depuis lors since then
derrière behind
dès from (*time*)
dès que as soon as
dessous underneath, beneath
ce-dessous below (this)
dessus on top
au-dessus (de) above

ci-dessus above (this)
devant in front (of)
doucement quietly; gently, softly
tout droit straight (on)
à droite on the right, to the right
dur: travailler dur to work hard
en effet indeed, as a matter of fact
également also; equally
encore still; again
encore une fois once again
enfin finally, at last
énormément (de) a lot (of)
ensemble together
ensuite then, next; later
entièrement entirely
entre between
environ about
éventuellement possibly, perhaps
évidemment evidently; obviously
exactement exactly
exprès on purpose, deliberately
à l'extérieur (de) outside
extrêmement extremely
face à facing; faced with
en face (de) opposite
facilement easily
de façon à so as to
fidèlement faithfully
finalement finally, in the end; after all

fort hard
franchement frankly, honestly
à gauche on the left, to the left
en général usually
généralement generally
gentiment nicely
grâce à thanks to
gravement gravely; seriously
ne . . . guère hardly
d'habitude usually
comme d'habitude as usual
par hasard by chance
au hasard at random
en haut (de) at the top (of)
de haut en bas from top to bottom
à l'heure on time
de bonne heure early
heureusement fortunately
hier yesterday
avant-hier the day before yesterday
ici here
immédiatement immediately
n'importe où anywhere
intellectuellement intellectually
à l'intérieur (de) inside
jadis formerly, once
jamais ever
ne . . . jamais never
jusqu'à until; as far as, up to
jusqu'ici so far, until now
jusque-là until then

justement exactly
là there
là-bas over there, down there
là-haut up there
légèrement slightly; lightly
le lendemain the next day
le lendemain matin the next morning
lentement slowly
loin (de) far (from), a long way (from)
le long de along
longtemps (for) a long time
lourdement heavily
depuis lors since then
maintenant now
mal badly
malgré in spite of, despite
malheureusement unfortunately
manuellement manually
au maximum at (the) most; to the utmost
même same; even
même pas not even
quand même even so
mentalement mentally
mieux better
le mieux best
au milieu de in the middle of
moins less, minus
moins de less than, fewer than
au moins at least (*quantity*)
du moins at least

mystérieusement mysteriously
naturellement of course, naturally
nerveusement nervously
normalement normally
notamment especially
de nouveau again
nulle part nowhere
ne . . . nullement in no way
où where
n'importe où anywhere
en outre furthermore
paisiblement peacefully
par by; through
par terre on the ground
par-dessous under(neath)
par-dessus over (the top) (of)
parfaitement perfectly
parfois sometimes
parmi among
à part apart (from)
nulle part nowhere
quelque part somewhere
en particulier in particular
particulièrement particularly
partiellement partially
à partir de from
partout everywhere
pas du tout not at all
pas loin de not far from
patiemment patiently
à peine scarcely, hardly, barely

pendant during, for
peu à peu little by little
à peu près about, approximately
peut-être perhaps, maybe
poliment politely
plus [plys] plus
en plus [plys] moreover
plus de (pommes) [ply] no more (apples)
plus de (dix) [ply] more than (ten)
de plus [plys] moreover
de plus en plus [dəplyzãply] more and more
ne . . . plus [ply] no more, no longer
plus tard [ply] later
non plus [ply] neither, either
moi non plus! nor me!
plutôt rather
pour for; in order to
pourtant yet, nevertheless
près de near (to)
à présent at present
presque almost, nearly
à proximité de near to
puis then, next
quand when
quand même however, even so, nevertheless
quant à (moi) as for (me)
quelquefois sometimes
quelque part somewhere
rapidement quickly

rarement rarely, seldom
récemment recently
régulièrement regularly
en retard late
sans without
sans cesse without stopping, ceaselessly
sauf except (for)
selon according to
sérieusement seriously
seul(e) alone
seulement only
simplement simply
soigneusement carefully
soudain suddenly
sous under
souvent often
"suite" "continued"
à la suite de following
suivant according to, following
"à suivre" "to be continued"
sur on
sûrement certainly, surely
sur-le-champ at once
surtout especially
sus: en sus in addition
tant de so much, so many
tard late
plus tard later
trop tard too late

tellement so; so much
de temps en temps now and then, from time to time
de temps à autre from time to time
en même temps at the same time
tôt early
trop tôt too soon, too early
le plus tôt possible as soon as possible
toujours always; still
en tout in all
tout d'abord first of all
tout à coup suddenly
tout à fait completely, quite
tout près (de) quite close (to)
tout de suite at once
à travers through
très very
trop too; too much
trop de too much, too many
uniquement only
un à un one by one
vers towards; about (*of time*)
vite quickly, fast
vraiment really
y there, to that place, in that place

SOME EXTRA NOUNS!

un accord ⇨ agreement
un accueil reception
l'action f action
l'activité f activity
l'âge m age
l'ambition f ambition
l'âme f soul
l'amour m love
l'angoisse f anguish, distress
une annonce advertisement
l'arrière m back, rear
l'attention f attention; see **faire**
à l'attention de for the attention of
un attrait attraction
un avantage advantage
une aventure adventure
un avis notice; opinion
à mon avis in my opinion
la bataille battle
le bâton stick
la beauté beauty
le besoin see **avoir**
la bêtise stupidity
le bien good
le bonheur happiness, good luck
la bousculade bustle
le bout end
le bruit noise
le but ⇨ aim; goal
le calme peace, calm
le candidat candidate
le caractère ⇨ character, nature; letter

le cas case
en cas de in case of, in the event of
en tout cas in any case
la catastrophe disaster
la cause cause
à cause de because of
le centre centre
le cercle circle
le chagrin distress
la chance luck
la chapelle chapel
le chapitre chapter
le charme charm
le chef ⇨ chief, head, boss
le chiffre figure; numeral
le choix choice
la chose thing
le chuchotement whispering
la civilisation civilization
le classement classification
le clocher steeple
le coin corner
la colère anger; see **mettre**
la colonne column
le commencement beginning
la comparaison comparison; see **soutenir**
le compte calculation
la confiance confidence
le confort comfort

la connaissance *see* **faire**

la conscience conscience

le conseil (piece of) advice

la construction construction

le contraire the opposite
au contraire on the contrary

la copie copy

la corbeille basket

le/la correspondant(e) correspondent

le coup blow, bang, knock

le courage courage, bravery

cours: au cours de during, in the course of
en cours in progress

la coutume custom

la crainte fear

le cri cry

la culture ⇨ culture

la curiosité curiosity

le danger danger

les débris wreckage

le début beginning

la décision decision

les dégâts damage

le désarmement disarmament

le désastre disaster

le désavantage disadvantage

le désir desire, wish

le désordre disorder

le destin destiny

le détail detail

la détresse distress

la déveine bad luck

le (bon) Dieu God

la différence difference
quelle est la différence entre X et Y? what is the difference between X and Y?

la difficulté difficulty

la dimension dimension

la direction direction

la discipline discipline

la dispute argument, dispute

la distance distance

le doute doubt
sans doute no doubt; probably

le droit right

la durée time

un échange exchange; *see* **taux**
en échange de in exchange for

l'économie *f* economy; saving

un effet effect

un effort effort

un électeur elector

une élection election

l'élégance *f* elegance

un endroit place

l'énergie *f* energy

l'engagement *m*: "**sans engagement**" "without commitment"

l'ennemi *m* enemy

l'ennui *m* annoyance, boredom
une enseigne sign
un ensemble group (*of buildings etc*)
l'enthousiasme *m* enthusiasm
un entretien conversation, discussion
envie *see* avoir
les environs *mpl* surrounding district
l'épaisseur *f* thickness
une erreur mistake
l'espace *m* space
une espèce sort, kind, species
en espèces in cash
un espoir hope
l'essentiel *m* the main thing
une étape ⇨ stage; stopping point
un état state
l'étendue *f* extent
l'étonnement *m* astonishment
un événement event
un excès excess
un exemple example
par exemple for example
l'exil *m* exile
l'expérience ⇨ *f* experience
un expert expert
une explication explanation
une exposition exhibition

un extrait extract
la fabrication manufacture
la façon way, method, manner
de cette façon in this way
le fait fact
la faute ⇨ fault
c'est de ma faute it's my fault
la fermeture closure
la fin end
la flèche arrow
la foi faith
la fois time
la folie madness
le fond background; bottom
la force strength
la forme form, shape
la foule crowd; heap
la fraîcheur freshness
les frais expenses
le franc franc
la gaieté, la gaîté gaiety
le genre type, kind, sort
la gentillesse kindness
les goûts interests
chacun son goût every man to his taste
le gouvernement government
grand-chose *nm/f inv*: **pas grand-chose** nothing much
la grandeur size
le gros lot first prize (*in lottery*)
le groupe group

la guerre war
le guide guide
l'habileté f skill
l'habitude see avoir
la :halte stop, break; halt
faire halte to stop
l'harmonie f harmony
le :haut-parleur (pl haut-parleurs) loudspeaker
la :hauteur height
l'honneur m honour
les honoraires mpl fees
la :honte shame
l'humeur f humour, mood
l'hygiène f hygiene
une idée idea
un/une idiot(e) idiot
une image picture
l'imagination f imagination
un/une imbécile idiot, imbecile
l'inconvénient m disadvantage
l'importance f importance
une impression impression
un/une inconnu(e) stranger
un inconvénient disadvantage
les informations fpl news
un inspecteur inspector
les instructions fpl instructions
l'intention f see avoir

l'intérêt m interest
une interruption break, interruption
une interview interview
la jalousie jealousy, envy
la joie joy
le jouet toy
le journal (pl journaux) newspaper
la largeur width
la larme tear
le lecteur reader
la légende caption
le lieu place; see avoir
au lieu de instead of, in place of
la ligne line
la limite boundary, limit
la liste list
la littérature literature
la livre (sterling) pound (sterling)
la location ⟡ hire, rental
le loisir leisure
la longueur length
la Loterie Nationale National Lottery
la lumière light
la lutte ⟡ struggle
le magazine magazine
la malchance bad luck
le malheur misfortune
la manière way, method
le manque (de) lack (of)
le maximum maximum
le mélange mixture
le membre member
la mémoire memory
la méthode method, way

le mieux best; *see* **faire**
le milieu centre, middle
le minimum minimum
le Ministère de the
   Ministry of
le mot word; note,
   message
sans mot dire without
   saying a word
le moyen (de) the
   means (of)
au moyen de by means
   of
le mystère mystery
négatif: au négatif in
   the negative
le niveau (*pl* **-x**) level
le nombre number
la nouvelle (piece of)
   news
une objection objection
un objet object
une observation
   remark
une occasion
   opportunity; occasion
les œuvres *fpl* works
une opinion opinion
un ordre order
l'orgueil *m* pride
l'ouverture *f* opening
la page page
la paire pair
le panier basket
le panneau (*pl* **-x**) sign,
   notice
le pari bet
la parole word
la part part

de la part de on behalf of;
   from
de ma part on my behalf;
   from me
pour ma part for my part
la partie ▷ part; *see* **faire**
le pas footstep
la patience patience
la peine difficulty
la pensée ▷ thought
la permission
   permission
la personne person
la phrase sentence
**la pièce (de 10
   centimes)** (10-centime)
   coin
la plaisanterie joke
le plaisir pleasure
le plan ▷ plan; map
au premier plan in the
   foreground
à l'arrière plan in the
   background
le plateau ▷ (*pl* **-x**)
   plateau
la plupart de *or* **des**
   most (of)
le poids weight
le point point, mark
le point de départ
   starting point
le point de vue point of
   view
la politesse politeness
la politique politics
**portée: à portée de la
   main** within arm's
   reach

le **portrait** portrait
positif: au positif in the positive
la **position** position
la **possibilité** possibilty, opportunity
la **poupée** doll
le **pouvoir** power
les **préparatifs** *mpl* preparations
la **préparation** preparation
la **présence** presence
le **pressentiment** feeling
le **principe** principle
en principe as a rule; in principle
le **problème** problem
le **produit** product; produce
la **profondeur** depth
le **projet** plan
la **propreté** cleanliness
la **prospérité** prosperity
les **provisions** provisions
la **prudence** caution
avec prudence carefully; cautiously
la **publicité** publicity
la **qualité** quality
la **question** question
le **raccourci** short-cut
la **raison** reason; *see* **avoir**
le **rapport** connection
la **religion** religion
les **remerciements** *mpl* thanks
le **remue-ménage** stir,

hullaballoo
la **rencontre** ⇨ meeting
le **rendez-vous** appointment; date; meeting place
les **renseignements** *mpl* information
la **réponse** reply
la **reprise** resumption
la **réputation** reputation
le **rescapé** survivor
le **réseau** (*pl* -**x**) network
la **résolution** resolution
le **respect** respect
les **restes** *mpl* remains
le **résultat** result
le **retour** return
de retour back
la **réussite** success
le **rêve** dream; dreaming
de rêve: une maison de rêve a dream house
la **révolution** revolution
le **révolutionnaire** revolutionary
le **rythme** rhythm
la **saleté** dirtiness
le **sang-froid** calmness
le **sanglot** sob
le **schéma** diagram, plan
le **secours** help
le **secret** secret
la **section** section
la **sécurité** security
le **séjour** stay
la **sélection** selection
le **sens** sense
la **sensation** sensation; *see* **faire**

la **série** series
le **service** service
de **service** on duty
le **signe** sign; *see* **faire**
le **silence** silence
le **sinistre** disaster
la **situation** situation
la **société** society
la **solution** solution
la **somme** sum
le **son** sound
le **sort** fate
la **sorte** sort, kind
le **soupçon** suspicion
le **sourire** smile
le **souvenir** souvenir
le **spectateur** spectator
le **style** style
le **succès** success
le **sujet** subject, matter
au **sujet de** about
la **surprise** surprise
la **surveillance** supervision; watch
le **système** system
la **tâche** task
le **talent** talent
le **taux de change** exchange rate
la **taxe** tax
la **tentative** attempt

le **terme** term, expression
le **texte** text
la **théorie** theory
la **timidité** shyness
le **tour** ⇔ turn; trick
c'est ton **tour** it's your turn
le **tournoi** tournament
la **trace** sign, trace
la **tragédie** tragedy
la **tristesse** sadness
le **tube** tube; hit song *or* record
le **type** fellow, chap, sort, kind
le **va-et-vient** coming and going
la **valeur** value
la **vapeur** ⇔ steam
la **veine** ⇔ luck
la **version** version
le **verso** back (of page)
la **victoire** victory
la **vie** life
les **vœux** *mpl* wishes
le **voyage** journey
la **vue** view
de **vue** by sight
en **vue de** with a view to

VERBS

abandonner to abandon
abîmer to spoil
aboutir to end
s'abriter to shelter
accepter to accept
accompagner to go with
accomplir to accomplish
s'accoutumer à to become accustomed to
accrocher to hang (up); to catch (*à* on)
accueillir to welcome
accuser to accuse
acheter to buy
achever to finish
acquitter to endorse
admettre to admit
adorer to adore
s'adresser à to apply to; to speak to
affecter (de faire qth) to pretend (to do sth)
afficher to display
affirmer to maintain, assert
agacer to irritate, aggravate
agir to act, behave
il s'agit de it is a question of
agiter le bras to wave
s'agrandir to grow
aider qn à to help sb to
aimer to like, love
aimer bien to like
aimer mieux to prefer
ajouter to add

aller to go
aller chercher qn to fetch sb, go and meet sb
aller voir to go and see
s'en aller to go away
allumer to switch on; to light
amener to bring; to bring about
s'amuser to enjoy oneself
annoncer to announce
s'apercevoir de to notice
appartenir (à) to belong (to)
appeler to call
s'appeler to be called
apporter to bring
apprécier to appreciate
apprendre (à faire) to learn (to do)
apprendre qch à qn to teach sb sth
(s')approcher de to approach
approuver to agree with; to approve (of)
appuyer to press; to lean (*object*)
s'appuyer to lean
arracher to pull out; to snatch; to tear
s'arranger: cela s'arrangera it will be all right
arrêter to stop; to arrest
s'arrêter to stop

arriver to arrive; to happen
s'asseoir to sit down
assister à to attend, be present at, to go to
assurer to assure; to insure; to ensure
attacher to tie, fasten
attaquer to attack
atteindre to reach
attendre to wait (for); to expect
attirer to attract
attraper to catch
augmenter to increase
(s')avancer to go forward
avoir to have
avoir l'air (de) to seem (to)
avoir besoin de to need
avoir chaud/froid to be hot/cold (*person*)
avoir envie de to want to
avoir l'habitude de to be in the habit of
avoir honte (de) to be ashamed (of)
avoir l'intention de to intend to
avoir lieu to take place, to occur
avoir du mal à to have difficulty in
en avoir marre to be fed up
avoir peur to be afraid
avoir raison/tort to be right/wrong

avouer to confess
baisser to lower
balbutier to stammer
barrer to block
bâtir to build
battre to beat
se battre to fight
bavarder to gossip, chat
bloquer to block
bouger to move
bouleverser to startle, shatter
bricoler to potter about, do odd jobs
briller to shine; to sparkle
briser to break, smash
brûler to burn
(se) cacher to hide
(se) calmer to calm down
casser to break
causer to cause; to chat
cesser (de) to stop
changer d'avis to change one's mind
chanter to sing
charger (de) to load with
chasser to chase (off); to get rid of
chauffer to warm up, heat up
chercher to look for; *see* **aller, envoyer**
choisir to choose
chuchoter to whisper
circuler (of vehicles)
cirer to polish

collaborer to collaborate
collectionner to collect
coller to stick
commander to order
commencer (à) to begin (to)
compenser to compensate for, make up for
comporter to comprise
composer to compose; to make up; to dial
composter to date-stamp; to punch
comprendre to understand
compter to count; to intend to
concerner to concern
conclure to conclude
conduire to drive
condamner to condemn; to sentence
se conduire to behave
confectionner to make
confesser to confess
confirmer to confirm
connaître to know (*person, place*)
consacrer to devote (*time*)
conseiller to advise
conserver to keep
(se) considérer to consider (oneself)
consister to consist
consommer to consume
constater to establish; to state
constituer to constitute, make up

construire: faire construire une maison to have a house built
consulter to consult
contacter to contact, get in touch with
contempler to contemplate
contenir to contain
continuer to continue
convenir to be suitable
copier to copy
se coucher to go to bed; to lie down
coudre to sew
couler to flow
couper to cut (off)
courir to run
couvrir to cover
craindre to be afraid of, to fear
créer to create
crever to have a puncture
crier to shout, cry
critiquer to criticize; to assess
croire to think; to believe
cueillir to pick; to capture
cultiver to grow, cultivate
danser to dance
se débrouiller to manage
décharger to unload
déchirer to tear
décider (de) to decide (to)
se décider (à) to make

up one's mind (to)
déclarer to declare
se décourager to
become discouraged
découvrir to discover
décrire to describe
défendre to forbid; to
defend
dégager to clear; to
extricate
se déguiser to disguise
oneself
demander qch à to ask
sb for sth
**demander à qn de faire
qch** to ask sb to do sth
se demander to wonder
demeurer to live
démolir to demolish
dépasser to overtake; to
exceed
se dépêcher to hurry
dépendre de to depend
on
**déplaire: cela me
déplaît** I don't like it
déposer to put down
déranger to disturb
désapprouver to
disapprove of
descendre to come or go
down; to get off (*train
etc*); to take down
désirer to desire, want
dessiner to draw
détester to detest
détourner to divert
détruire to destroy
développer to develop

devenir to become
devoir to have to (*must*)
différer (de) to differ
(from), be different
(from)
diminuer to diminish,
reduce
dire to say, to tell
à vrai dire as a matter of
fact
diriger to direct
se diriger vers to go
towards
discuter to discuss
disparaître to disappear
se disputer to argue,
have an argument
distinguer to distinguish
distribuer to distribute
diviser to divide
dominer to overcome; to
dominate
donner to give
donner sur to overlook
dormir to sleep
doter (de) to endow
(with)
se doucher to have a
shower
douter (de) to doubt,
have one's doubts
about
dresser to set up, erect
se dresser to stand (up)
durer to last
échanger to exchange
s'échapper (de) to
escape (from)
éclairer to light (up)

éclater de rire to burst out laughing

économiser to save

écouter to listen (to)

écraser to crush

s'écraser to crash

s'écrier to exclaim, cry out

écrire to write

effectuer to carry out

effrayer to frighten

s'élancer to rush, dash

élever to erect; to raise

s'élever to rise

(s')embrasser to kiss

emmener to take

empêcher (de) to prevent (from)

employer to use; to employ

emporter to take; to carry

emprunter qch à qn to borrow sth from sb

encourager qn à faire to encourage sb to do

s'endormir to fall asleep

enfermer to imprison

s'enfuir to flee

enlever to take away; to get rid of; to take off

s'ennuyer to be *or* get bored

enregistrer to record

ensevelir to bury

entasser to stack

entendre to hear

qu'entendez-vous par . . .? what do you mean (*or* understand) by . . .?

entendre parler de to hear about

s'entendre to agree, get on

entourer (de) to surround (with *or* by)

entrer (dans) to enter, go *or* come in(to)

envahir to invade

envelopper to wrap (up)

envoyer to send

envoyer chercher qn to send for sb

éprouver to experience, feel

espérer to hope

essayer (de faire qch) to try (to do sth)

essuyer to wipe

établir to establish, set up

étaler to spread out

éteindre to put out, extinguish; to switch off

(s')étendre to extend; to stretch out

étonner to astonish

s'étonner to be astonished

étouffer to suffocate; to be stifled

être to be

être assis(e) to be sitting

être obligé(e) de to be obliged to

être de retour to be back

être sur le point de to be on the point of, be just about to

être en train de faire

qch to be (busy) doing sth
étudier to study
(s')éveiller to wake up
éviter (de faire) to avoid (doing)
exagérer to exaggerate; to go too far
examiner to examine
s'excuser (de) to apologize (for)
exister to exist
expliquer to explain
exprimer to express
fabriquer to manufacture, make
se fâcher to become angry
faillir: il a failli tomber he almost fell
faire to do; to make
faire attention to be careful
faire chaud/froid to be hot/cold (*weather*)
faire la connaissance de to meet
faire entrer quelqu'un to let somebody in
se faire couper les cheveux to have one's hair cut
faire du mal (à) to harm
faire de même to do the same
faire partie de to belong to (*club etc*)
faire de son mieux (pour) to do one's best (to)

faire une promenade to go for a walk
faire remarquer to mention, point out
se faire remarquer to be noticed
faire semblant de to pretend to
faire sensation to cause a sensation
faire signe to signal, wave
il faut one must *etc*
falloir to be necessary
féliciter to congratulate
(se) fermer to close, shut
fermer à clef to lock
figurer to imagine
finir to finish
fixer to stare at; to fix
flâner to stroll, lounge about
fonctionner to work
faire fonctionner to operate
former to form
fouiller to search
fournir to provide
frapper to hit, strike, knock
fréquenter to frequent (*place*); to see (*person*)
gagner to win; to earn
garantir to guarantee
garder to keep
gâter to spoil
se gâter to go wrong
gémir to groan
gêner to bother

glisser to slip, slide
gratter to scratch
grimper to climb
guetter to watch
habiter to live (in)
hésiter to hesitate
heurter to bump into
ignorer not to know
imaginer to imagine
imprimer to print
indiquer qch à qn to inform sb of sth
s'inquiéter to worry
ne vous inquiétez pas! don't worry!
inscrire to inscribe
s'inscrire to register
installer to fix (up)
s'installer to settle, sit (down)
s'instruire to educate oneself
insulter to insult
interdire to prohibit
"interdit de fumer" "no smoking"
intéresser to interest
s'intéresser à qch to be interested in sth
interroger to question
interrompre to interrupt
interviewer to interview
introduire to introduce
inviter to invite
jeter to throw (away)
joindre to join
jurer to swear
laisser to leave; to let; to allow

laisser tomber to drop
lancer to throw
(se) laver to wash
lever to lift; to raise
se lever to get up; to stand up
lire to read
loger (chez) to lodge (with), live (with)
louer to hire, rent
lutter to struggle
manœuvrer to manoeuvre; to operate
manquer to miss; to be lacking
marcher to walk; to work (of object)
se marier (avec qn) to marry (sb)
marquer to mark; to write down; to score
mêler to mix
se mêler (à qch) to be involved (in sth)
menacer to threaten
mener to lead
mentir to lie, tell a lie
mériter to deserve
tu l'as mérité! you deserved it!
mesurer to measure
mettre to put (on); to take (time)
mettre qch au point to bring sth about; to get sth ready
mettre qn à la porte to throw sb out
mettre qch à la poste

to post sth
se mettre à l'abri to take shelter
se mettre en colère to get angry
se mettre en route to set off
monter to come *or* go up; to get into (*car etc*); to take up
montrer to show; to point out
se moquer de to make fun of
multiplier to multiply
noter to note
nourrir to nourish; to cherish
obliger qn à faire to force *or* oblige sb to do
observer to observe; to keep
obtenir to obtain
s'occuper à to occupy oneself *or* keep oneself busy (with)
s'occuper de to attend to; to be concerned with
offrir to give, offer
s'opposer à to be opposed to
ordonner to order, command
organiser to organize
orner (de) to decorate (with)
oser (faire qch) to dare (to do sth)
oublier to forget

(s')ouvrir to open; to switch on
paraître to appear
parier (sur) to bet (on)
parler to speak, talk
partager to share
participer (à) to take part in; to share in
partir to leave, depart, go away
à partir de from
passer to pass; to spend (*time*)
passer un examen to sit an exam
se passer to happen
passionner to excite
pavoiser to decorate with flags
payer to pay
peindre to paint
pénétrer (dans) to enter, make one's way into
penser (à) to think (about)
penser de to have an opinion of
perdre to lose
perdre qn de vue to lose sight of sb
permettre (à qn de faire) to allow *or* permit (sb to do)
persuader to persuade
peser to weigh
photographier to photograph
placer to place, put

se plaindre (de) to complain (about)
plaire (à) to please
cela me plaît I like that
plaisanter to joke
pleurer to cry
plier to fold
porter to carry; to wear; to take
poser to put (down)
poser des questions to ask questions
posséder to possess
poursuivre to pursue
pousser to push; to grow
pousser un cri to utter a cry
pouvoir to be able to (*can*)
pratiquer to go in for
précipiter to hurl
se précipiter dans to rush into
prédire to predict
préférer to prefer
prendre to take; to have
prendre feu to catch fire
prendre part à to take part in
prendre qch à qn to take sth from sb
prendre soin (de) to take care (to)
préparer to prepare
présenter to present; to introduce
se présenter to appear; to introduce oneself
prêter qch à qn to lend sb sth

prévoir to foresee
prier to request
je vous en prie please, don't mention it
priver qn de qch to deprive sb of sth
produire to produce
se produire to happen, occur
profiter (de) to take advantage (of)
se promener to go for a walk
promettre (à qn de faire qch) to promise (sb to do sth)
prononcer to pronounce
prononcer un discours to make a speech
proposer (de faire) to suggest (doing)
protéger to protect
protester to protest
prouver to prove
provoquer to cause
se quereller to quarrel
quitter to leave
raccommoder to mend, repair
raconter to tell
ralentir to slow down
ramasser to pick up
ramener to bring *or* take back
ranger to arrange, tidy
se rappeler to remember
rapporter to report; to bring back
rater to miss; to fail

rattraper qn to catch up with sb
recevoir to receive
réchauffer to warm (up)
recommander to recommend; to register (*letter*)
recommencer to begin again
reconnaître to recognize
recouvrir (de) to cover (with)
reculer to move back; to reverse
redescendre to come *or* go down again
refaire to re-do, do again
refermer to close again
réfléchir to think, reflect
refuser (de) to refuse (to)
regagner to go back to
regarder to look (at)
régler to adjust; to direct (*traffic*); to settle (*bill*)
regretter (que) to be sorry (that)
rejoindre to meet; to rejoin, to reach
se relever to get up again
relier to connect
relire to read again
remarquer to notice
rembourser to refund
remercier (de) to thank (for)
remettre to put back; to take back; to postpone

remonter dans to get back into
remplacer to replace
remplir (de) to fill (with)
remuer to stir
rencontrer to meet
se rencontrer to meet; to collide
rendre to give back
rendre visite à to visit
se rendre to surrender, give oneself up
se rendre à to visit (*place*)
se rendre compte to realize
(se) renfermer to shut (oneself) in
renseigner to inform
se renseigner (sur) to inquire (about)
rentrer to return
renverser to overturn, knock over
renvoyer to send back
réparer to repair
repasser to press, iron
répéter to repeat
répondre to reply
se reporter à to refer to
se reposer to rest
reprendre to resume
représenter to represent
réserver to book, reserve
résoudre to resolve
respecter to respect
ressembler à to resemble

ressortir to bring or take out
rester to stay, remain
retenir to book, reserve
retentir to sound
retourner to return
se retourner to turn round
retrouver to meet; to find (again)
se réunir to meet
réussir (à faire) to succeed (in doing)
se réveiller to waken up
révéler to reveal
revenir to come back
rêver to dream
revoir to see again
au revoir goodbye
rigoler, rire to laugh
risquer (de) to risk
rougir to blush
rouler to drive (along)
saisir to seize, grasp; to catch, understand
salir to dirty
saluer to greet
sauter to jump
sauver to save
se sauver to run off
savoir to know (fact)
sécher to dry
secouer to shake
sélectionner to select
sembler to seem
sentir to smell
se sentir (mal) to feel (ill)
séparer to separate

se serrer la main to shake hands
(se) servir to serve (one-self)
se servir de qch to use sth
signaler to point out
signer to sign
sonner to ring
sortir to go or come out; to take out
se soucier de to worry about
souffrir to suffer; to bear, stand
souhaiter to wish
soulager to relieve
soulever to lift
soupçonner to suspect
soupirer to sigh
sourire to smile
soutenir la comparaison avec to bear comparison with
se souvenir de qch to remember sth
sucer to suck
suffire to be sufficient
suggérer to suggest
suivre to follow
supposer to suppose
à supposer que . . . supposing that . . .
surprendre to surprise
sursauter to give a jump
se taire to be quiet
tâter to taste; to sample

téléphoner (à) to telephone
tendre to hold out
tenir to hold; to run (*shop*)
tenter de to attempt to
(se) terminer to finish
tirer to pull; to let off (*fireworks*); to shoot
tomber to fall
laisser tomber to drop
tomber en panne to break down
toucher (à) qch to touch sth
toucher de l'argent to receive money
tourner to turn; to shoot (*film*)
se tourner vers to turn towards
traduire to translate
trahir to betray
traîner to drag, pull
travailler to work
traverser to cross; to go through; to go over
tromper to outwit
se tromper to be mistaken
troubler to worry
trouver to find
se trouver to be (situated)
tuer to kill
unir to unite
utiliser to use
vaincre to conquer
valoir to be worth
vendre to sell
venir to come
venir de faire qch to have just done sth
vérifier to check
verser to pour
visiter to visit
vivre to live
voir to see
voler to steal; to fly
vouloir to want
vouloir bien (+ *infinitive*) to be happy to
vouloir dire to mean
voyager to travel

The following French words have more than one translation, depending on context. If you do not already know these translations, check them up on the pages shown.

un **accord** 142, 217
les **affaires** *fpl* 35, 127
une **aiguille** 177, 179
l'**air** *m* 10, 30, 58, 62, 74, 86, 198
une **ampoule** 115, 127
l'**argent** *m* 134, 138, 150, 160
un **avocat** 36, 100
le **bac** 70, 158, 196
la **baie** 101, 155, 159, 191
le **bain** 124, 156
le **balcon** 116, 120, 170
le **ballon** 166, 194
la **bande** 99, 115, 131, 135
la **barrière** 59, 83, 121, 153, 189
le **bâton** 60, 142
la **batterie** 41, 51, 143
la **bibliothèque** 35, 103, 163, 183
le **billet** 10, 96, 128, 170, 186
(le) **bleu** 48, 114
le **bœuf** 14, 82, 88
la **boîte aux lettres** 125, 129
le **bouton** 44, 64, 118, 124
le **buffet** 102, 186
le **bureau** 32, 70, 102, 180, 202
le **but** 166, 217

le **cadre** 36, 104
le **café** 88, 160
la **caisse** 43, 129, 161
la **canne** 47, 59, 169
le **caractère** 50, 64, 217
le **carnet** 66, 182, 186
la **carrière** 35, 61
la **carte/les cartes** 31, 67, 75, 89, 97, 203
le **chasseur** 58, 118
le **chauffeur** 38, 188
le **chef** 34, 92, 118, 217
la **cheminée** 123, 159
le **client/la cliente** 116/ 117, 160/161
le **coffre** 40, 102
la **coiffeuse** 35, 105
la **colle** 73, 141, 179
le **concours** 70, 98
la **corbeille** 127, 173, 218
la **corde** 139, 143, 179
le **costume** 44, 170
la **côte** 19, 25, 75, 93, 157, 201
la **cour** 71, 123
la **course** 165, 169
la **crème** 93, 113
la **cuisine** 67, 121, 203
la **cuisinière** 31, 35, 103, 125
la **culture** 153, 218
la **dame/les dames** 79, 99
le **décor** 122, 172

la **défense** 17, 137, 169
le **directeur/la directrice** 66/67, 116/117
la **discothèque** 97, 127
la **distribution** 131, 173
le **drap** 124, 140, 202
une **écharpe** 47, 115
un **employé/une employée** 32/33, 128, 160/161
une **entrée** 11, 89, 117, 121, 171, 187
une **expérience** 17, 67, 219
la **faute** 67, 135, 219
le **fils/les fils** 78, 130
le **filet** 168, 188
la **galerie** 43, 185
le **garçon** 78, 88, 116, 202
le **gardien** 30, 136
la **gelée** 95, 201
la **glace** 31, 89, 103, 125, 102, 199
le **glaçon** 94, 200
le **grenier** 84, 122
le **guichet** 128, 170, 186
l'**hôtel** *m* 116, 180
l'**informatique** *f* 51, 79
le **jean** 44, 138
le **jeu** 96, 166, 170
les **jumelles** *fpl* 61, 81, 159, 173
la **langue/les langues** 23, 67
le **linge** 46, 126, 202
le **livre/la livre** 66, 129, 148

la **location** 173, 220
la **loge** 123, 173
la **lutte** 169, 220
le **maillot** 44, 156, 168
le **mannequin** 36, 164
le **marché** 160, 180
(le) **marron** 48, 100
le **mécanicien** 32, 38, 186
la **mort/le mort** 29, 40, 41, 134, 135
le **mouton** 14, 82, 92
la **note** 69, 117, 143
un **orchestre** 142, 170
une **ordonnance** 113, 137
la **paille** 85, 95, 141
le **parking** 38, 120, 180
le **parterre** 154, 172
la **partie** 148, 167, 221
la **pâtisserie** 89, 161
le **patron/la patronne** 32/33, 90
le **pavillon** 122, 154, 158
le **pays** 52, 58, 74, 82, 198
la **pêche** 101, 167
la **peinture** 99, 103, 127
la **pelle** 159, 179
la **pensée** 155, 221
le **pensionnaire/la pensionnaire** 72 118/119
le **phare** 40, 158
le **pic** 20, 178
la **pièce** 103, 121, 129, 171
le **pilote** 12, 34
la **piste** 13, 169

The vocabulary lists on the following pages cover all of the nouns in the first two levels of the book, i.e. ESSENTIAL and IMPORTANT, and will be a useful translation guide when you have a mental blank.